UNLOCKING CITY HALL
EXPLORING THE HISTORY
OF LOCAL GOVERNMENT AND POLITICS

Exploring Community History Series Editors

David E. Kyvig
Myron A. Marty

Unlocking City Hall
Exploring the History of Local Government and Politics

Michael W. Homel

KRIEGER PUBLISHING COMPANY
MALABAR, FLORIDA
2001

Cover photo: Providence, RI, City Hall, 1900. Library of Congress, LC-D4-19706

Original Edition 2001

Printed and Published by
**KRIEGER PUBLISHING COMPANY
KRIEGER DRIVE
MALABAR, FLORIDA 32950**

Copyright © 2001 by Michael W. Homel

All rights reserved. No part of this book may be reproduced in any form or by any means, electronic or mechanical, including information storage and retrieval systems, without permission in writing from the publisher.
No liability is assumed with respect to the use of the information contained herein.
Printed in the United States of America.

FROM A DECLARATION OF PRINCIPLES JOINTLY ADOPTED BY A COMMITTEE OF THE AMERICAN BAR ASSOCIATION AND A COMMITTEE OF PUBLISHERS:
This publication is designed to provide accurate and authoritative information in regard to the subject matter covered. It is sold with the understanding that the publisher is not engaged in rendering legal, accounting, or other professional service. If legal advice or other expert assistance is required, the services of a competent professional person should be sought.

Library of Congress Cataloging-in-Publication Data

Homel, Michael W. (Michael Wallace), 1944–
  Unlocking city hall : exploring the history of local government and politics /Michael W. Homel.
    p.   cm. — (Exploring community history series)
  Includes index.
  ISBN 0-89464-987-6 (pbk : alk. paper)
    1. Local government—United States—History. 2. Municipal government—United States—History. I. Title. II. Series.

JS309 .H65 2001
320.8'5'0973—dc21

00-059947

10 9 8 7 6 5 4 3 2

To local elected officials in North America
and to their campaign supporters

CONTENTS

Editors' Introduction	ix
Acknowledgments	xiii
Part I Opening the Door	
1. Investigating Local Government and Politics	3
2. Connecting the Past and Present	6
Part II Examining Local Government	
3. Looking Around City Hall	25
4. Probing the History of Local Government Services	50
Part III Exploring Local Politics	
5. Uncovering the History of Urban Politics	97
6. Tracing Local Campaigns and Elections	127
Part IV Displaying Results	
7. Illuminating City Hall	153
Index	163

EDITORS' INTRODUCTION

Government, any of a variety of mechanisms with granted or assumed power to order or assist human activity, is an essential characteristic of life in communities. A completely solitary life may only require self-reliance and self-discipline. But once humans associate with others, they seek some efficient means of coordinating their desires for predictability, security, and other mutual benefits. Whether it involves domination by the biggest and strongest, deference to inherited authority or religious or economic power, or some sort of shared decision making, government functions to allocate resources, supervise behavior, punish offenses against accepted standards, and provide aid to some or all of those within its jurisdiction. Despite occasional calls from the far left or far right to dispense with it, government of some sort has been almost universally accepted as a necessary feature of human society.

Ancient Greeks referred to the community of persons with some role in government, those empowered to participate in making choices about the nature of government together with those involved in its conduct, as the polity. Thus the process of considering alternatives and making decisions respecting government, whatever the nature of that process might be in particular circumstances, came to be known as politics. Government and politics, therefore, go hand in hand as central elements of any community's collective experience.

The politics and government of every community intertwine with its particular identity. Communities vary according to place, population, and circumstance, and they change over time. Each community, given its distinctive character, setting, and unfolding circumstances, possesses a unique past. In order to understand the nature of a community at present, not to mention at any time in its past, comprehending the history of that community's government and politics becomes vital. This book provides guidance to those who recognize the value of such knowledge, who desire to acquire or enhance it, and who wish to do so efficiently, effectively, and thoroughly.

Most communities instinctively know that their own particular history is important to them. Recalling nothing of that past puts them in the same position as people suffering from amnesia, unable to remember their origins, their response to needs or challenges, their means of achieving success or dealing with setbacks, their sources of support or opposition, and their goals. History serves the community much as memory serves an individual. In imperfect, sometimes distorted, but most often helpful fashion both memory and history help identify familiar elements in new situations and provide a guide to appropriate behavior. History also offers a standard of comparison across stretches of time and circumstance that exceeds the span of an individual life. In this sense, history is far more than a remembrance of things past. History represents a means of coming to terms with the present, developing an awareness of previous influences, the continuities and distinctiveness in current conditions, and the range of future possibilities. Just as memory helps the individual avoid having to repeat the same discoveries, behaviors, and mistakes, historical knowledge helps a community, as well as any group or individual within it, avoid starting at the beginning each time an issue needs to be addressed.

Even if there is obvious value to a community in understanding its own history, the means of acquiring such self-knowledge are usually less evident, especially when the subject of interest is previously unexamined. Knowledge of the past is commonly gained from books, teachers, museums, films, or other presentations. What is one to do if the subject has never been explored, if there is no book on the topic in the library, if there is no expert to whom to turn? What is to be done in the even more likely circumstance that answers obtained from such sources are insufficient or unsatisfying?

A number of years ago, we began to appreciate that many people would like to explore the past of their own families and communities. Only the lack of research knowledge and confidence stood in their way. We realized from working with undergraduate students, local historical and genealogical societies, and out-of-school adults that any literate person motivated to explore some question regarding the past of his or her immediate surroundings could master most historical research methods, pursue most research possibilities, critically evaluate most potential explanations, and achieve a considerable measure of understanding. We felt it important to empower people to function as historians themselves or evaluate what other historians might say and write about a personally important past.

We began our effort to identify questions of historical significance and interest as well as explain how to investigate them in *Your Family History: A Handbook for Research and Writing* (Arlington Heights, IL: Har-

Editors' Introduction

lan Davidson, 1978). Four years later we continued the undertaking with a larger book, one more widely focused on communities. *Nearby History: Exploring the Past Around You* (Nashville, TN: American Association for State and Local History, 1982) was, nevertheless, merely a general overview to a broad and complex subject. The warm reception which greeted *Your Family History* and *Nearby History* encouraged us to carry our notion further by providing specific advice on exploring particular topics. Enlisting historians who were experts on schools, homes, public places, places of worship, and businesses, we edited a five-volume nearby history series, originally published by the American Association for State and Local History and currently available from AltaMira Press of Walnut Creek, California. We have been pleased to be able to expand the scope of these efforts through a series of books devoted to exploring community history produced by the Krieger Publishing Company, the first two of which were Ann Durkin Keating's *Invisible Networks: Exploring the History of Local Utilities and Public Works* and R. Douglas Hurt's *American Farms: Exploring Their History.*

The book before us is an important addition to the *Exploring Community History* series. *Unlocking City Hall* considers the structures and functions of local government and politics in North America. Most significant, it describes ways to pursue an inquiry into the history of these matters in either United States or Canadian communities. The book is filled with ideas about topics and issues well worth examining, shrewd suggestions about how to go about such an investigation, and useful examples of successful previous inquiries that may provide models and inspiration.

We asked Michael W. Homel to write this guide to exploring the history of local government and politics based on long acquaintance and respect, but in particular because he possesses an extraordinary background. Mike Homel is, first of all, a well-recognized scholar of such matters, the author of a valuable study of Chicago school politics, and a long-time professor of history at Eastern Michigan University. In addition, he is an experienced practitioner in the field about which he writes, having served as both a city council member and mayor of Ypsilanti, Michigan. We believe his book displays both the vision of a thoughtful scholar and the down-to-earth wisdom of a veteran of local government and politics. *Unlocking City Hall* should be a useful tool to anyone—interested citizen, beginning or advanced student, or engaged participant in local government and politics—seeking a deeper understanding of a community's vital history.

David E. Kyvig, Editor
Myron A. Marty, Consulting Editor

ACKNOWLEDGMENTS

This book owes its life to David Kyvig, Professor of History at Northern Illinois University. David has effectively promoted the study of local history both among academic historians and those outside the universities. David suggested that I write this book and remained undeterred by my evasions while I held local elective office. Once I took on this project, David's graceful combination of responsiveness, patience, encouragement, and wisdom proved highly valuable.

I thank Eastern Michigan University, my home for three decades, for a sabbatical leave which gave one semester's respite from an ample teaching load and enabled me to move ahead with writing. Lester B. Scherer, a model colleague in so many ways, generously read the manuscript and made suggestions which I readily incorporated. Matthew Farkas, a graduate student of unusual vigor and outstanding ability, helped with research.

I appreciate the cooperation of Julianne Ruby, Cascade County (Montana) Historical Society; Billie Zolkosky, Ypsilanti Historical Museum; and the staffs at the Chicago Historical Society and Bentley Historical Library of the University of Michigan. David Siegel, Department of Politics, and Joseph Kushner, Department of Economics, both of Brock University in Ontario, Canada, answered my questions about Canadian politics and government.

It has been a pleasure to work with the people of Krieger Publishing Company. Their mix of warmth, enthusiasm, communication, and professional skill reassured me at every turn. Senior Editor Mary Roberts is a master at the difficult task of care and feeding of authors. Editor Elaine Rudd zestfully adopted the manuscript as her own, displaying attention to detail and navigating me through seemingly never-ending production steps. The excitement Mary and Elaine had about this project was so important in reminding me that it was worth the time and energy it took.

PART I

OPENING THE DOOR

Chapter 1

INVESTIGATING LOCAL GOVERNMENT AND POLITICS

North Americans are deeply ambivalent about both government and politics. In the wake of Vietnam, Watergate, Iran-Contra, and scandal from the county courthouse to the White House, we are more cynical than confident about government. According to the current fashion, government is costly, wasteful, ineffective, and oppressive. Suspicion of government, however, is not just a recent gust in a politically conservative climate. From our earliest days, we have been wary of government and have therefore limited its scope and divided its powers. But our feelings about government are mixed. Over the years, we have demanded that government do more and more. From promoting economic prosperity to suppressing offensive behavior, from assuring old-age security to teaching children to drive, our expectations of government have steadily risen, even as we doubt that it can act wisely and well.

Our hostility toward politics is even stronger. We regard politics as corrupt and corrupting, something good people avoid. We use the word "political" to denounce, not to describe. We see political conflict as petty and unnecessary, not as the way society makes decisions. Candidates for public office assure voters they are not "career politicians." And we enact term limits in case they change their minds after we elect them. Our most beloved public figures are those we believe are "above politics." Busy with our private lives, few of us attend public meetings, write letters to newspapers, contact government officials, or assist election campaigns. A majority of our eligible voters do not even vote; our election-day turn-out is well below that of a century ago or of other nations today. Nevertheless, politics fascinates us. Broadcasters and journalists give it a lot of attention, and we talk about it at work and with friends. The excitement of many such discussions suggests that, even as we condemn politics, it matters a lot to us.

Both government and politics should mean much to us. Through government we try to maintain order, decide what to do in common, and deliver services to the community. Through government we specify how we will provide public services, who will get them, and who will pay for them. Through politics we designate those who will wield public power, at least until the next election. Moreover, through politics we make public decisions, whether for the entire nation or for a single state or locality. These decisions may affect our lives, sometimes dramatically so.

Indeed, local politics and government normally touch our daily routines more than the national events news media emphasize. As we drive on nearby streets, send our children to school, walk at the neighborhood park, or turn on the kitchen faucet, we meet local government. We take its presence for granted. If, however, snow drifted over winter streets, uncollected trash piled at our curb, or firefighters or police did not come quickly in an emergency, we would be furious. Meanwhile, local politics sets directions for where we live. Should vacant land be developed? If so, should it have stores, apartments, or houses? Should gays and lesbians have equal access to jobs, housing, and public places? Should we recycle garbage or bury it in a landfill? Should we buy a new fire engine or build a recreation center? Should we give tax breaks to lure a new factory? Each of these choices is important; each has its own fascinating tale. This book tells how to unlock the compelling stories of how our cities, townships, counties, and districts maintain order, furnish services, and make decisions.

Learning about local government and politics can nourish a sense of place and community identity. It is a way for both long-time residents and new arrivals to strengthen bonds to their neighbors and to their home towns.

Second, probing local politics and government is a good way to pursue almost any interest we have. For example, local historians can learn how society makes decisions by researching an election campaign or how a city council or county board makes policy. Furthermore, those interested in broad national issues can examine them in local settings. Whether their passion is for small business, environmental quality, technological change, or women's rights, why not learn about them through the lens of their own community? Or a researcher can consider the impact of a national event, such as the Great Depression, Cold War, or Red Scare through a local case study.

Third, some use local governmental or political history to become more involved in community affairs. Some hope to solve a particular problem, such as preserving a historic landmark or halting home burglaries. Others want to help a friend or neighbor run for office. Still others find their interest in the history of the local library leads to service on the library board. After all, if individuals do not make their voices heard, those who do not share their goals and values may well make decisions for the community.

Besides its inherent human interest, the history of local government and politics can enrich understanding of today's problems. History, after all, addresses how people react to situations, what decisions they make, and how well such decisions work out. For example, knowing how local government responded to a flood, hurricane, or tornado in the past may help a community in future disasters. Familiarity with arguments and choices about downtown parking or disorderly youth in the past will mean more useful responses when such issues surface again. Using the past to make better decisions for the future is called policy history.

Anyone can figuratively unlock the doors of city hall to learn more about local government and politics. We all know enough to begin asking questions. Unlike many fields of knowledge, the sources, methods, and language of history are accessible to all who have the time and interest. Most local history sources are close at hand, right in our own community. And the immediacy of local history sparks interest.

This guidebook provides know-how for students and teachers, public officials, reporters and editors, archivists, museum workers, and residents who want to do the history of local government and politics. It comments about the process of doing history. It suggests many possible topics and offers questions to ask about these topics. It points readers toward raw materials useful for exploring community history. Finally, it indicates a number of ways one can present one's findings.

Chapter 2

CONNECTING THE PAST AND PRESENT

Awareness of local government and politics makes some people curious about their history. History is the recorded human past that historians select, organize, and present in a meaningful way. Animals, plants, and inanimate objects all have pasts, but only people have history. History serves compelling human needs. It explains our own lives and the world around us. History also helps construct individual, family, and group identities. In addition, historical understanding shapes present-day opinions and actions. For some, a sense of the past means support for the way things are; for others, it justifies change.

Many regard history as remote and irrelevant. For them, "history" is a school class or museum visit, but such things are detached from "real life." This view stems from regarding history as dramatic national or world events and actions of "great men" like Lincoln, Napoleon, and Hitler. Such a definition of history, though, is too narrow. History is about all of us, and it is always close at hand. History lies in our memories of the past, our questions about why things are the way they are (and if they should be different), and in our encounters with ideas, institutions, relationships, and the material world previous generations left us. We encounter history in many ways. Some, like a local heritage fair, a historic district like Seattle's Pioneer Square, a Civil War novel, or movies about the western frontier, explicitly derive from the past. But even everyday experience, which we rarely regard as "historical," rests on our understanding—often unstated and unquestioned—of the past.

Making history starts with questions about the past. Sometimes others choose the questions. For example, a teacher may assign a paper or class presentation on the impact of the Vietnam War on a community. Or when a Congressional committee schedules hearings on farm policy, the U.S. Department of Agriculture may instruct its historians to write a paper about past outcomes of crop price supports. Current events and social trends can also prompt questions about the past. The surge of work on technological, environmental, welfare, minority, gender, and women's history in recent years shows this. Questions arise from personal experience as well. A reader who grew up in Irvine, California, starts thinking about her childhood and decides to find out more about Orange County in the 1970s and 1980s. Another reader's parents moved from Mexico, first to south Texas, then to Dallas. Learning about their experiences deepens his understanding of them and of himself. Whether our questions arise from the news or quests for self-discovery, when we probe the past we better understand the present.

These same motives shape questions about the history of local government and politics. A University of Wisconsin student wonders how Madison changed after eighteen-year-olds began voting in the 1970s, owing to the Twenty-Sixth Amendment to the U.S. Constitution. Meanwhile, in Calgary, Alberta, a retired firefighter makes a public library display about the history of his department to honor his colleagues and tell the public about how they served the community. Any current or recent political or governmental issue, be it a budget crisis, ethnic or racial conflict, or proposed new highway, justifies the perspective and understanding that comes from historical study.

History, like other human endeavors, can be disputed. Although historians often see things the same way, this is not always the case. One reason why they may differ about the past is that they use different sources or value sources differently. Suppose three people wrote about Charles Stenvig's 1969 mayoral election in Minneapolis. How did each use newspapers? Interviews? Election returns? Census data? Photographs? Radio and television archives? Records of Stenvig's campaign? His opponent's? Each account may differ, depending on its sources. New evidence can yield new conclusions. Previously unknown or inaccessible materials may surface. Or one historian may use evidence others overlooked or disregarded.

Even with identical sources, researchers may disagree about the past. Slavery, the Holocaust, and Hiroshima still provoke fierce debate, though each event took place long ago. While local history has a smaller canvas, it too, has controversies, some of them intense. For example, two local historians may write conflicting accounts of a town's decision to rezone land for a new WalMart. Each may be fair and accurate, but differing views about economic development can bring them to opposing conclusions about the same evidence. For this reason, whether you read original sources or historical accounts, always consider authors' perspectives while forming your own judgments.

As noted earlier, the questions historians ask also shape their results. Different historians ask different questions. They respond to shifting public concerns. Their inquiries also arise from their backgrounds and experiences. Questions they ask change over time, as new generations experience life differently. Also, whereas history was once the property of an affluent few, these days people of diverse backgrounds do history and claim it as their own. Some observers resist such change and reject the new perspectives it brings. They rail at "revisionists" and embrace as The Truth what they believed history was at some unspecified time in the past. But if history did not speak to our concerns, it would be fossilized and irrelevant. Both professional historians and the public will continue to ask questions, and these questions will lead to new understandings of the past.

There are many ways to arrange local history. A chronological account may come to mind first, but other ways of organizing the past can be equally or more fruitful. Some history seems best suited to a topic or subject-matter organization. Other times, comparative studies are most enlightening. The historian can cover a broad time span, choose one significant limited period, or select several important eras, a technique called "post holing." Consider organizing decisions carefully. They determine a project's time and expense, and they also shape the results of one's labors. Also, although it is usually possible to change a research plan, doing so can be inefficient.

One practical way to answer questions about the past is to investigate a specific event or episode. Doing so provides sharp focus and limits research time. For example, suppose a researcher observes that certain people or groups in a community have political influence. He or she may wonder why this is true and how it came to be. One way to answer the question would be to examine one or more election campaigns or to trace the enactment of an ordinance or policy by city council or township board to learn who determined the outcome. As always, the questions determine the path of research. For example, a New Englander affected by factory closings of the 1980s may want to find out how Manchester, New Hampshire, coped with the Great Depression. Meanwhile, an Ontario resident interested in government may ask how Toronto changed when John Sewell was mayor in the late 1970s.

Researchers also answer questions about political power by writing the history of a local organization or institution. Perhaps the Chamber of Commerce, United Auto Workers, or Christian Coalition is prominent in an area's politics. Why not trace that group's rise or probe its role in an important episode? Other nongovernmental groups to study might include political parties and caucuses, neighborhood associations, civic clubs, churches, and informal cliques like the Wednesday morning coffee club at Shoney's Restaurant. Local government agencies are also suitable for historical study. These include both administrative departments, like police, fire, parks, and recreation, and legislative bodies like city councils or township or county boards. Students often overlook decision-making bodies that apply the law, such as zoning and planning commissions or municipal and county courts. Because such institutions often maintain records, they can be fertile fields for local historians.

Research on particular persons who have left their mark on the community is another pathway to the past. A question about political power can lead to a noted elected official, political party leader, or public administrator such as an engineer, police chief, or city manager. Another local historian, asking different questions, may study people who functioned outside the spotlight. The lives and work of public employees who cleaned streets, put out fires, and processed invoices reveal much about any area's past. Either individual or group biography finds eager audiences.

A fourth type of topic is how a community responded to a long-term problem or issue. How did Duluth cope with massive winter snowfalls? How did Los Angeles deal with ever-increasing demand for water? How did whites and blacks in Richmond, Virginia, set rules for race relations after the Civil War? During civil rights protests of the 1950s and 1960s? During recent litigation on affirmative action? Issue-oriented or problem-based history speaks directly to practical problems and thus interests policy-makers.

No matter whether historians approach the past through incidents, institutions, individuals, or issues, our efforts must have limits or boundaries. Although there are no easy formulas for this, it is well to avoid certain pitfalls. A huge scope of time and space may overwhelm the researcher and end with a superficial result. On the other hand, tiny boundaries can limit audience appeal. Happily, researchers can narrow or broaden work as it evolves. A local historian agrees to do a library display on twentieth-century Memphis politics but half-way through realizes there is neither time nor space for such an ambitious effort. Instead, the researcher does one panel each on the 1910s, 1930s, and 1960s, or narrows the work even more by comparing Edward H. Crump's mayoralty (1910–1916) to present-day concerns. On the other hand, with additional effort, historians can broaden a topic if it proves too narrow.

Whatever the boundaries, it is important that questions about the past determine both research and writing. As one does research, lots of interesting information appears, and it is tempting to display most of it. But yielding to that temptation costs history its purpose and focus. Although it is often advisable to change questions along the way, let those questions, not the evidence encountered, guide the work. Keeping questions uppermost ensures distinction between what is useful and that which, however enticing, is irrelevant to the goal. Placing top priority on your questions also exposes gaps in evidence you should fill. And a clearly defined purpose will attract readers or viewers and hold their interest.

Whatever the questions about local government, it is well to keep its basic structure in mind. In the United States and Canada, local governments originate from states or provinces. U.S. cities and some townships operate under state-approved charters, while most Canadian cities function under provincial municipal acts. Counties and most townships in both countries get their authority directly from state or provincial law, as do regional governments in Canada. If a student chooses to study the history of a local government's framework, the following questions may be useful: What is its structure? What goals and values does it reflect? What does it reveal about the times in which it was written? Under what circumstances did the government's charter come into being? Who wrote it? How did the author or authors get their authority? What alternatives, if any, did they consider? Why did they make the choices they did? What was the process for charter approval? If it required voter enactment, what did the campaign and election reveal about community politics? Some students of city charters use a comparative approach. How does the structure of this city or township government compare with other nearby communities? With cities or townships farther away? What explains similarities and differences? Some regard city charters as dusty and abstract. As with national constitutions, however, each clause of a charter has its own story, and often it is a lively one.

ॐ ॐ ॐ ॐ ॐ

WRITING CITY CHARTERS: WHAT'S AT STAKE

Sacred symbol or power grab? Representative democracy or rule by the ignorant? Efficiency or class privilege? Though debates about local government charters may focus on structure, they are not merely theoretical. They are really about political and economic power.

Here is a selective guide about what to look for when studying a municipal, township, or county charter. Are the government's powers broad or narrow? Pay close attention to taxation, regulation, and authority to provide services. Second, what is the balance of power between executive and legislative branches? Is there a chief executive officer? Is he or she elected or appointed? Does that official have veto and appointment power? How long are elected officials' terms? Does the charter limit the number of terms they may serve? Third, how is representation decided? Is it based on land, such as one county commissioner per township? Or is it based on population? Do voters elect representatives from districts? Or from the entire jurisdiction as a whole ("at large")? Fourth, notice the role of political parties. Are local elections partisan or nonpartisan? Do elections occur when voters choose state and national officials? Or are local elections held separately? Has the charter changed over time? If so, how and why? Using the records of charter commissions, the press, and, if possible, interviews, your study of one government's framework can reveal a compelling story of local history.

ॐ ॐ ॐ ॐ ॐ

On the other hand, local historians may be more interested in the people in local government. The candidates inviting residents to campaign fundraisers, the clerk who processes building permits, the crew cutting grass and trimming trees in the park—these are the faces of local government. Perhaps a family member worked for the township or county. Or the researcher may be a public employee or a potential candidate for office. In any of these cases, some questions may come to mind. What backgrounds did elected officials in this area have? Why did they run for office? How did they get elected? What explains their political successes and failures? How did public service change their lives?

Perhaps questions are about local politics. As later chapters of this book show, possibilities for historians abound. As suggested earlier, they could study one or more of the many political groups in your community. Document and assess their membership, issues, methods, successes, and failures. Or a researcher may investigate a single area's political "system." For example, how significant were issues in a community? If so, which ones? How important were personal or factional fights? What role did political parties play? How well-organized were they? Did a single party dominate or did two or more

Employees of tax assessor's office with residents on tax review committee, Great Falls, Montana, 1899. What were the backgrounds of public administrators and their employees? How did they get their jobs? What were their career patterns? How did their jobs differ from those in business or in private nonprofit agencies? *Courtesy of the Cascade County Historical Society.*

political parties compete? Did local politics attract lots of people or just a few? If the latter, who took part and were they different or similar from the population as a whole? Did elections settle differences, evade them, or consist of continual battles over the same things? What was the connection between national events and local politics? How has local politics changed over time? These are a few of the doorways historians of local politics can open.

By now one may have some questions about local government and politics and may be thinking about how to answer them. Consider the available evidence. With local history, most sources are close at hand. It may not be necessary to travel to distant archives, although researchers may need to use libraries at a nearby university, large city, or state or provincial capital. In these places, they not only examine sources but also meet the people who care for them. At public libraries, government and newspaper offices, historical societies, and local museums, archivists are proud of their collections and eager to help. To make a research visit successful, define goals as specifically as possible and respect each facility's regulations.

Campaign wagon for city council candidate, Chicago, 1903. This glimpse of a local campaign raises questions about gender and political participation. Who were these men and boys? What were they doing and why? *Chicago Historical Society, Photo Files, ICHi-30843.*

Historians classify sources as primary and secondary. Primary or original sources are records contemporaneous to the events you study or evidence contemporaries later produced (such as memoirs or autobiographies). A Galveston, Texas, police officer's diary from 1900 is a primary source for research about that city's massive flood. The 1900 U.S. census and contemporary newspaper reports and charity agency records are also primary sources. Besides written materials, primary sources include such things as photographs, buildings, and objects of daily life. Secondary sources, meanwhile, come from those without first-hand experience. For example, a 1912 Galveston newspaper story written by a journalist not in the city during the flood and a 1967 *American Heritage* article about the flood are secondary sources.

The same source may be both primary and secondary, depending on the subject. For example, the transcript of an interview with a retired township supervisor in Dodge County, Nebraska, is a primary source for his recollections about how World War II changed his rural community. When, however, this former official talks about his area's nineteenth-century settlement or comments on recent quarrels among township board members he read about in the newspaper, his words become a secondary source. And the *American Heritage* article on the Galveston flood can be a primary source for those analyzing the historical profession in the 1960s. Historians normally use both primary and secondary sources. The latter offer valuable background and perspective, identify primary sources, and have evidence you may not get elsewhere. Nevertheless, it is best to rely mainly on primary sources, since they give the most direct and detailed view of the past.

Historians approach sources with both respect and skepticism. Sources are links to the past, and many are rare or unique. Researchers should use each carefully, leaving it in the same place and condition as they found it so others may consult it, too. At the same time, every historical source came from a person or group that created it for some reason. Accordingly, view it critically and resist the tendency to accept it at face value. For every source, primary or secondary, published or unpublished, written or visual, ask questions to gauge its reliability. Who created this evidence? What do you know about them? What were their opinions, and how did these views shape the document? When did they create the source? Under what conditions? For what purpose? What was the source's relationship to your topic? One needs to make independent judgments about sources, not parrot them uncritically. Assess sources using common sense, knowledge of human nature, and sources' internal consistency. Historians also try to corroborate information from at least two independent sources. In sum, use the same critical intelligence toward records of the past as you do for evidence in your daily life.

Government records may be the most important primary sources. At city or township halls or county buildings, they may be in the department that produced them or in central sites, such as a clerk's office, municipal reference library, warehouse, or basement. Some governments give records to a nearby public library, historical society, college, or university. No uniform retention standards exist for local government records. Some governments keep a great deal, especially where historical consciousness is strong, like New England. Others readily discard material they believe has no practical use but takes up valuable space. Often chance determines survival. Fires, floods, and insects robbed us of some of our past, while in other cases individuals who cared about history saved records from furnace flames or garbage dumps.

Government records vary in their purpose and characteristics. Some, such as annual reports or newsletters, were intended for wide distribution. Others, like minutes of meetings, election returns, property deeds, probated wills, and birth, death, and marriage certificates, established formal public records. Even documents with identical purposes vary widely. Some meeting minutes record details of discussions, but others merely report votes on motions, resolutions, and ordinances. Some public reports have abundant information, while others are brief, general, and sanitized.

Other government documents were generated for internal use, not public consumption. These include building permits; tax assessment cards; voter registration files; records of police calls, dog licenses, and housing inspections; and a wide range of unpublished reports, correspondence, and internal memos. They document everything from antiprostitution campaigns in San Francisco to tuberculosis patients in Otter Tail County, Minnesota. They range from the killing of a native American in Providence, Rhode Island, in 1676 to gas and oil leases in early twentieth-century Cherokee County, Oklahoma. Such records not only document a community's past but also reveal how local government and politics functioned. Court files, for example, trace crime, personal conflicts, and business disputes but also show how police, judges, and juries operated. Documents produced for internal use may reveal disagreements and options that sources issued for public consumption omitted. For this reason, both types of sources can be profitable.

Government records, like other sources of the past, have changed over time. Researchers of eighteenth- or nineteenth-century history rely on written evidence and physical artifacts. In the twentieth century, however, people increasingly spoke by telephone and rarely saved evidence of their conversations. By the end of the twentieth century, computer e-mail messages became common, and officials rarely saved these either. But researchers of the recent past have some compensations. The volume of written materials remains large, despite phones and e-mail. Historians can interview participants and use audiotapes or videotapes of public meetings. Moreover, since the 1970s, freedom of information laws in many jurisdictions permit public access to many government records.

Newspapers are a second major primary source local historians use. College, university or public libraries, historical societies, and newspaper offices are likely places to find them. Some exist in bound volumes, others on microfilm or microfiche. There may also be scrapbooks and clipping files. One can order newspapers unavailable locally through interlibrary loan. Wise researchers consult not only local dailies and weeklys but those published in nearby communities as well. Metropolitan areas also have neighborhood and suburban newspapers along with major dailies. In some places, gay and lesbian, black, ethnic, and foreign-language publications are valuable sources. Newspapers are essential for local history. Reading them is time-consuming, and one can readily became entranced by advertisements and sports and crime accounts. But the press yields lively, contemporary accounts and often includes evidence missing from public documents.

On the other hand, historians must use newspapers cautiously, remaining alert to selectivity, accuracy, and bias. Like other humans, publishers, editors, and reporters had opinions. Their views helped determine what stories they covered and what they said. Thus, it is wise to consider the purpose of each newspaper story. "The news" was not simply a report of what occurred; it often reflected a journalist's or official's aim to promote or oppose a policy, group, or individual. In other words, the press did not simply report what happened; it shaped events as well.

In addition to newspapers, other periodicals may be helpful. Consider nationally circulated magazines of news and opinion. For the early twentieth-century United States, for example, head for *Survey, World's Work, Outlook, McClure's, Harper's Weekly,* and *Century,* among others. If your focus is on the 1950s and 1960s, *New Republic, Nation, Christian Century,* and *National Review* are good sources. Although these magazines reported most often on large cities, they sometimes covered medium-sized or small communities. Some magazines specialize in urban issues. *National Municipal Review, American City, Nation's Cities,* and *Governing* followed government at various times in the twentieth century, while *Campaigns and Elections* has illuminated the political process. Canadian researchers, too, will find both general interest magazines like *Maclean's* and *Actualities* and urban-focused journals like *Municipal World*. Specialized topics have their own publications. Police, fire, historic preservation, public works, parks—all have professional organizations with newsletters or journals. *Readers' Guide to Periodical Literature* and *Social Science and Humanities Index* (twentieth century) and *Poole's Index to Periodical Literature* (nineteenth century) are finding aids for many magazines and journals but do not include everything. Internet search engines and on-line indexes help with late twentieth-century publications.

It is always wise to identify unpublished nongovernmental manuscript materials about a community and to learn whether they can help answer questions. Which people and organizations in a particular area saved correspondence, financial records, reports, pamphlets, flyers, press clippings, and photographs? Did they keep such material in their own homes or offices? By asking around, local historians may locate and gain access to such evidence. Were manuscript materials donated to a library or historical society? If so, experienced researchers discuss their projects with an archivist. He or she can describe manuscript collections and explain how they are organized. Archivists also specify rules, including how to handle materials and take notes, and whether donors restrict publication. As with newspapers, writers must often look over much manuscript material to uncover a few valuable nuggets.

Researchers dealing with the last half-century can speak with those who experienced the past first hand. Through inquiries and written records, they can find people willing to answer questions about local government and politics. Besides prominent persons, historians should talk to lesser-known people, such as public employees and residents. Some may confirm existing knowledge, while others may offer new perspectives; all will enrich the result. Interviews require preparation. It is best to exhaust print sources before interviewing because well-informed interviewers set their own agenda instead of simply reacting to respondents. Prepared interviewers also react skillfully to what informants say. Interviews give evidence unavailable elsewhere, but they require the same questions and caution as print sources. Remember, too, that memories of the past are often inaccurate, either because they have faded or because people want to see the past in a particular way. Nonetheless, even inaccurate memories have value. The suggested readings at the end of this chapter lead to advice about interviewing and oral history.

City directories and local, state/provincial, and federal censuses can identify lesser-known people and add data about those encountered in other sources. City directories, published by private firms, list names, occupations, and race in street-address order. Directories make it possible to determine the occupation of a candidate for office or learn where firefighters tended to live. The local historian can also do a social profile of a neighborhood. Manuscript census lists are also well-suited for these purposes. National censuses every ten years in the United States and Canada not only counted population but described it in detail. Census takers sought to record each person's name, age, address, race, and occupation. They also asked residents about birthplace, property ownership, and household relationships. Except for the destroyed 1890 manuscript census, original U.S. federal census lists are made available on microfilm after seventy-two years. Statistics Canada maintains its nation's census records. In addition to manuscript lists, published aggregate census data covers counties, cities, and parts of large cities. State and local governments sometimes compiled censuses, too. Neither censuses nor city directories are complete or entirely accurate. Nevertheless, both give important information about individuals, neighborhoods, and communities, and prudent historians make good use of them.

Maps provide a physical sense of a community's past. They identify political jurisdictions and electoral districts, and document tax assessors' operations, transit service, street networks, and other aspects of government. Maps are commonly mixed with other sources, but some libraries and archives have separate map collections. The 300,000 fire insurance maps made by the Sanborn Map Company for 3,500 different cities make up an outstanding twentieth-century archive. For example, the Sanborn maps include 278 Pennsylvania cities from 1935–1990.

Other visual sources, such as photographs, engravings, and paintings, also enrich local histories of government and politics. Libraries, historical societies, and newspaper archives hold visual evidence of the past. Like the printed word, photos, paintings, and drawings were the purposeful work of individuals. Accordingly, it is well to ask the same questions of visual as of printed sources. Who created the image? When and why? What is the image's perspective, composition, and lighting? How does it portray people? What objects and structures appear? What is omitted? What statement does the illustration make? What subjects abound in visual documents? What subjects are rare? What do you conclude from this?

Historians also use artifacts. Firefighting equipment, street lights, political signs and banners, and kitchen utensils all enhance our sense of the past. Each object has its own story, from origins and usage to the point at which people discarded or preserved it. The history of an artifact, such as a voting machine or traffic light, could make a worthy project. Some objects find homes in museums. Others remain in private hands or appear for sale in antique stores or auctions. Still others continue to serve their original function. Structures and environments also document the history of local government and politics. The

This pair of city council photographs from the same community about thirty years apart documents major political change. *Ypsilanti Historical Archives.*

recently completed county office building, the abandoned dump on the edge of town, large city parks, neighborhood play lots, and the former fire station now used as a restaurant all are opportunities awaiting the historian of local politics and government.

Thorough research requires that in addition to primary sources, one should use secondary work relevant to a project. Articles and books written by those who came before provide evidence, ideas, and leads to other sources. Unpublished M.A. theses and Ph.D. dissertations may also help, if their narrow focus is appropriate. The work of community-based amateur historians may also be useful. Academic scholars, such as historians, political scientists, or sociologists, have likely either published books or articles on the local community or offer relevant background for research. Public or college and university librarians can help find such secondary material.

Secondary sources are especially good for connecting a specific topic to its larger setting. This is especially important in local history, whose practitioners sometimes become enmeshed in the specific and particular and thereby lose context and perspective. That is why writers should aim to balance local distinctiveness with regional, national, or even international trends. For example, work on a small Mississippi town in the 1890s should reflect familiarity with cotton farming, populism, and race relations derived from secondary sources. Likewise, those who study government or politics in Akron, Ohio, in the 1930s need to set their story against the background of the Great Depression, the rubber industry, and the birth of the United Rubber Workers. Secondary sources call for the same questions asked of primary documents. Who was the author? When was the work written and published? Who published it? What sources did it use? What sources did it neglect? What judgments did it make? Are these conclusions convincing?

Besides visiting historical societies and libraries, researchers can look to the Internet for pertinent sources. Material available on the World Wide Web is increasing at a dizzying rate, with the Library of Congress, National Archives, universities, and historical museums making collections and exhibits accessible. One excellent example is the Library of Congress American Memory site; a single collection here contains some 25,000 photographs taken by the Detroit Publishing Company from 1880–1920 which document urban life. Guides cited in the bibliography take you to other sites.

This chapter began to address ways of thinking about the history of local government and politics. It raised questions about the past and considered how to define topics in local history. Then it identified broad categories of subjects that historians of local government and politics can consider. Finally, this discussion began to explore the kinds and locations of sources for research projects. The next step is to go to city hall or the county building to see what it looks like and who is inside.

SUGGESTED READINGS

David E. Kyvig and Myron A. Marty, *Nearby History: Exploring the Past Around You* (Nashville, TN: American Association for State and Local History, 1982; 2nd ed., Walnut Creek, CA: AltaMira Press, 2000); Carol Kammen, *On Doing Local History: Reflections on What Local Historians Do, Why, and What It Means* (Walnut Creek, CA: AltaMira Press, 1995); and Carol Kammen, ed., *The Pursuit of Local History: Readings on Theory and Practice* (Walnut Creek, CA: AltaMira Press, 1996) are three fine introductions to local history. A hands-on guide to maintaining and using public records is H. G. Jones, *Local Government Records: An Introduction to Their Management, Preservation, and Use* (Nashville, TN: American Association for State and Local History, 1980). Two indexes to manuscript collections are National Historical Publications and Records Commission, *Directory of Archives and Manuscript Repositories in the United States* (Phoenix, AZ: Oryx Press, 1988), and Library of Congress, *National Union Catalog of Manuscript Collections* (available on-line at Archives USA database <www.chadwyck.com> These guides, though, are not complete. Willa K. Baum, *Oral History for the Local Historical Society* (Nashville, TN: American Association for State and Local History, 1974/1), and Barbara Allen and Lynwood Montell, *From Memory to History: Using Oral Sources in Local History Research* (Nashville, TN: American Association for State and Local History, 1981), cover interviewing and preserving the results. Fire insurance maps from the Sanborn Map Company archives are available on microfilm from University Publications of America, Bethesda, Maryland, or on paper from the Sanborn firm in Pelham, New York. Two introductions to the Internet are Andrew Harnack and Eugene Kleppinger, *Online! A Reference Guide to Using Internet Sources* (New York: St. Martin's Press, 1998), and Dennis A. Trinkle and Scott A. Merriman, *The History Highway 2000: A Guide to Internet Resources* (2nd ed., Armonk, NY: M. E. Sharpe, 2000).

PART II

EXAMINING LOCAL GOVERNMENT

Chapter 3

LOOKING AROUND CITY HALL

Whatever specific questions a researcher asks about the history of local government, it is well to begin with its type, structure, and duties. Audiences will better appreciate the significance of what they see or read if they learn something of how government is organized, what it does, and how it relates to other governments nearby. Most areas have scores or even hundreds of local governments, and few can readily say how they all fit together. Moreover, categories of local government vary from place to place, so the picture given here does not fit every locality.

Municipal government is the most local. Municipal governments may be cities, towns, or villages. How do these differ? Which category applies to the community in question? Typically, municipalities get their authority from state-issued charters in the United States and from provincial municipal acts in Canada. Municipal governments can pass local laws (called ordinances), regulate a wide scope of behavior, and furnish services to residents. Townships, another category of local government in the United States and some parts of Canada, are unincorporated areas encompassing land outside municipalities. Townships are subdivisions of counties; traditionally, townships operated under state and county law, were mainly rural, and provided few public services. In many places, this pattern remains. In others, however, residential and commercial development has caused townships to behave like municipalities. Many acquired state-granted charters and today offer a similar array of services as municipalities.

Counties are the largest units of local government in the United States and much of Canada (parishes in Louisiana). Counties perform land-related transactions, handling deeds, tax assessment, and tax collection. Counties also run courts and record vital information (births, deaths, marriages, and divorces). In addition, counties have customarily furnished a few public services like policing and road construction and maintenance to unincorporated areas. In the last half-century, many counties have enlarged their duties, and today they conduct municipal functions in urban and suburban areas. Here they operate parks and recreation programs, libraries, and public health facilities. They also do police patrols and support services, send rescue vehicles, and collect and dispose of solid waste. Meanwhile, in some of Canada, regional governments have assumed duties counties handle in the United States. Examining the structure and scope of county or regional government or picking a single function to study can provide much useful information. Likewise, there can be value in analyzing the politics and finances of a decision to expand or reduce county or regional services. There is also benefit from probing the relationship between a county or region and one or more local units of government.

In addition to cities, townships, counties, and regions, many communities have special purpose districts that deliver specific services to multiple municipalities. Such districts are more common in the United States than Canada, where regional government in certain areas makes these districts unnecessary. In the United States, however, by the early 1990s, over 28,000 special purpose districts provided libraries, parks, mass transit, water and sewers, airports, mosquito abatement, schools, and other public activities. Some serve relatively small areas, while others spill over county and state borders. Early examples of special purpose districts include the Massachusetts District Commission (sewage, parks, and water, 1889–1895), the Chicago Sanitary District (water and sewage, 1889), and the Cleveland Metropolitan Park District (1917).

Despite their large budgets and essential functions, special purpose districts are nearly invisible to the public. Their governing boards are frequently appointive. Local news media typically ignore them, except for scandal or dramatic conflict. Nevertheless, these governments are well worth attention. Under what circumstances was a local special district established? Why didn't existing governments do the job? What are the district's main sources of revenue and spending? How are governing authorities selected? What policy choices have they made? With what results? How have they balanced local autonomy and regional efficiency?

Another way to explore the tension between efficiency and autonomy is to consider metropolitan government. In the United States, Miami, Nashville, Jacksonville, and Indianapolis have either created metro government or redefined and at least partly consolidated city and county government. In Canada, Winnipeg's Unicity, Metro Toronto (replaced by the new City of Toronto), and Ottawa-Carleton exemplify this trend. Has the area being studied considered merging local governments? Why or why not? Who favored and who opposed this change? Why? What role did partisan, economic, or sociological differences play? Were differing tax rates and levels of public services in different jurisdictions important?

Although metropolitan government has been rare in North America, it proves that local government boundaries are subject to change. This, too, can be the focus of inquiry. Perhaps in the local area two or more separate municipalities have merged. This occurred with the creation of New York City in 1898, but there are many lesser-known cases, too. Annexation is another form of municipal consolidation. In this case, a municipality absorbs adjacent unincorporated land or existing towns or villages. On the other hand, people also create more government units, as when residents establish new municipalities in unincorporated areas or when parts of an existing town or city break off to form a new one. Did a community experience annexation, the creation of new governments, or the abolition of existing ones? If so, why did this change take place? Who supported and who opposed the decision? What arguments did each side use? Did these arguments reflect or conceal actual motives? What was the legal framework for the change? And who determined that framework? Was public consent required?

Local historians might also explore relationships among different governments. Such interaction has political, financial, and legal or structural dimensions. They can use certain episodes as case studies or examine a time period. What is there to learn, for example, about relations between the subject municipality and others nearby? About the connections between this city or township and its county?

City-state or city-provincial relations are another fertile field. Through statutes and charters, states and provinces defined powers of local government, enabling or restricting what cities and townships could do. Local officials often complained that states weakened city governments and interfered in local affairs. State officials replied that city ineptitude or corruption justified a short leash. What authority did the state or province give and withhold from municipal governments? What disputes arose over these matters? A second aspect of local-state relations stems from the fact that local governments get a substantial share of their revenue from the state. What formulas determined state/provincial payments to a specific city or township? What state grants supported certain projects? Did each branch of state or provincial government treat the city or township the same? Did the state deal with large cities differently from small ones? Did regional variations exist within a province or state? Explain the findings.

Some researchers may be more interested in links between local and federal government. In the nineteenth-century United States, these involved customs houses, Indian reservations, post offices, and a few military facilities. Beginning in the 1930s Great Depression, federal-local interaction grew substantially. President Franklin Roosevelt's New Deal created public service jobs for the jobless. To revive the economy, Washington also funded much public-sector construction. Some cities received federal money for low-income housing projects. Later, Washington transformed communities by increasing home ownership through mortgage guarantees and loans to World War II veterans.

The New Deal altered local government as well. New buildings and infrastructure permitted city hall to do more. Federal requirements for data and planning made cities and counties more professional and bureaucratic. Cities banded together and lobbied for federal aid, launching the U.S. Conference of Mayors. Finally, as we shall see later, partisan politics changed, too. Historians, however, remind us that in many places, much remained as before. Officials threatened by change rejected federal programs or limited their effect. What mark did the New Deal make on local government and public services in your community? Apply one of the topics mentioned here to the locality under investigation. Did the Great Depression and New Deal change this community or did things stay about the same?

Those interested in more recent history have abundant opportunity to learn how federal activity shaped localities. What military production or military bases existed in a community? How did they affect public services and politics? In the 1950s and 1960s, the U.S. government launched slum clearance and urban redevelopment or urban renewal. Cities leveled "blighted" areas and built housing, corporate and public offices, civic and sports arenas, hospitals, and universities. These projects were sometimes controversial, as economic development advocates tangled with residents defending neighborhoods from demolition.

Massive expressway construction was another major federal initiative of the 1950s, 1960s, and 1970s. As early as the 1930s and 1940s, cities and states began to build limited-access highways. In the United States, the 1956 Interstate Highway Act accelerated expressway projects, since the federal government paid nine-tenths of the cost. Where are such roads located in your community? Why? Who determined their locations? What was the public's participation in this decision? How did the expressway affect existing property and future development patterns?

Historians and politicians still debate the consequences of federal urban, antipoverty, and welfare measures of the 1960s. A writer can join this dispute by assessing his or her community's experience. President Lyndon Johnson's War on Poverty, headed by an Office of Economic Opportunity (OEO), launched a barrage of urban initiatives in job training, education, legal aid, and volunteer public service. OEO's Community Action Program tried to empower the poor and funded social service, employment, and education projects in low-income neighborhoods. Meanwhile, the Model Cities program channeled federal dollars to city governments for projects in these same fields. And Washington expanded public housing and subsidized privately owned low- and moderate-income housing. Which of these Great Society programs operated locally? Who ran them? What did they do? What successes, failures, and controversies occurred? What light does this historical experience shed on current public policy debate?

Beginning in the late 1960s, U.S. federal urban policies turned in a different direction, and one can investigate some aspect of that. President Richard Nixon and a Democratic Congress ended many Great Society programs. Under the "New Federalism" slogan, Washington shifted from earmarking funds for specific programs to revenue sharing, in which local governments used federal dollars as they wished within broad categories. Revenue sharing and the Community Development Block Grants (1974) also changed how much money different places received. By weighting population more and social distress less, aging large cities got fewer dollars and suburbs, small towns, and Sunbelt cities got more. Did your community receive revenue sharing funds? Why or why not? How much? Who decided how the funds were used? What did they buy? With what results? What happened to the programs of the 1960s?

Those wanting to pursue still more recent history will find audiences interested in how U.S. federal policy in the 1980s affected local governments. How did cities respond to the end of revenue sharing and reduced federal money for housing, jobs, and mass transit? What was the fiscal and political impact? Did communities try Urban Development Action Grants or enterprise zones, through which government helped private investment in cities? Assess the outcome of such ventures.

Another dimension to national-urban relations is the routine federal presence in a community. It may be considerable. For example, are there regional federal offices? How many people do they employ? Does a community have federal prisons, Veterans' Administration hospitals, military bases, and/or aircraft or weapons factories? Perhaps a regional federal record center or presidential library operates nearby. What impact do these facilities have on local governments? Is the federal presence in your locality likely to grow or decline?

Another way to trace local government history is through its impact on the landscape. Historians can, for example, consider government buildings—city or township hall, county courthouse, police and fire station, water or sewage treatment plant, or public library. Or they can focus on public spaces—plazas and squares, streets, parks, or landfills. What do these structures and places suggest about the community that built or installed them? Did officials value modernity or tradition? Local distinctiveness or standardization? Exclusivity or inclusion?

Government presents itself to the public partly through its buildings. It is possible to choose one and write its history. When was it constructed? Who built it? Why? Did people disagree about the need for the building, its design, or location? If not, what does this indicate? If so, what do such conflicts reveal? How much did the structure cost? How did government pay for it? Notice where the public building is located. What does its site say about community development? About people's feelings toward government? The Jasper County Courthouse in Newton, Iowa, built about a century ago, occupies the middle of a large square at the center of town. By contrast, Saline, Michigan, placed its recently opened public library on the edge of town near empty land that homes and stores soon would fill. Each location reflects different values. Finally, does a structure stand alone or in a group of public buildings? Cleveland's City Hall (1912–1914) sits amid at least a half dozen large federal, county, and city buildings. What did city officials say when they made this locational decision?

Now consider the public building itself. Does it still serve its original function? Has its purpose changed over time? Sometimes local governments acquire a structure formerly used for something else. Miami City Hall, for example, began as a Pan American Airways terminal in the early 1930s. Twenty years later, Lafayette, Louisiana, turned a Sears department store into its municipal building. Does a structure have a specialized or multipurpose use? What is its architec-

Streetscape, Georgetown, Kentucky, 1996. Sidewalks, streets and street markings, lights, trash barrels, and apparently contradictory signage all illustrate the presence of local government. What are the stories and meanings behind these public artifacts? *Photo by author.*

Teton County Courthouse, Choteau, Montana, 1996. *Photo by author.*

tural style? What statements do its design and ornamentation make? Some buildings recall classical Greece or Rome; others evoke colonial America; still others imitate contemporary homes or offices. Enter a township hall or county courthouse. Notice its interior design, decoration, and use of space. A century ago, huge lobbies, tall ceilings, and grand stairways conveyed the majesty of government. What do today's public buildings say? Does a public building express local identity? The below-street-level council chamber in Scottsdale, Arizona's City Hall, for example, echoes the kiva, southwestern native Americans' ceremonial space.

City Hall, Browning, Montana, 1996. This pair of public buildings documents conflicting views about government and differing architectural styles over time. *Photo by author.*

ॐ ॐ ॐ ॐ ॐ

PUBLIC MONUMENTS

One way local governments define themselves and their communities is through monuments. Commemorative arches and statues make fine sources for local historians. Writers should observe them in a community, research their history, and consider their meanings. What events and people do they honor? What episodes and people are omitted? What designs did public officials adopt? What are their messages? Monuments can link past and present in telling ways. In 1890, Richmond, Virginia, authorities designated the continuation of Franklin Street as Monument Avenue, and erected a statue of Confederate General Robert E. Lee there. Over the next thirty years, city officials honored secession and southern independence by placing memorials to other Confederate heroes along this fashionable residential street.

By the 1990s, however, white flight to the suburbs and the civil rights movement made Richmond a different city. A black governor, Douglas Wilder, presided at the state capitol and a black mayor, Leonidas Young, sat in city hall. African Americans, noting that only three of sixty-five Richmond monuments honored blacks, called for racial diversity among Monument Avenue statues. In 1995, citizens argued about

Statue of Confederate Major General J. E. B. Stuart, Monument Avenue, Richmond, Virginia, ca. 1906–1910. *Library of Congress, LC-D4-36658 DLC.*

putting a statue of Richmond-born African American tennis player Arthur Ashe near Old South heroes. Supporters felt an Ashe statue would symbolize racial harmony or show black political power. But some whites did not want any black among Confederate greats. Meanwhile, certain blacks wanted Ashe honored in a black-oriented public place, not where he was unwelcome in life. In the end, City Council authorized a twelve-foot statue depicting Ashe with books, tennis racket, and admiring children on historic Monument Avenue.

Sources: Paul S. Dulaney, *The Architecture of Historic Richmond* (2nd ed., Charlottesville: University Press of Virginia, 1976); Jo Ann Tooley, "Boulevard of Broken Dreams," *U.S. News and World Report*, 111 (Nov. 11, 1991), p. 24; and several 1995–1996 articles in *New York Times, Jet,* and *Ann Arbor News.*

ॐ ॐ ॐ ॐ ॐ

Inside public buildings are the people of local government: citizen members of boards and commissions, administrators, salaried and

Looking Around City Hall

Ann Arbor, Michigan, City Council at work, 1956–1957. *Guy C. Larcom Papers, Box 10, Bentley Historical Library, University of Michigan.*

hourly employees, and, of course, elected officials. The history of each group merits study. A good starting point is with appointed boards and commissions. Most governments have many such committees. As news media usually ignore them, few realize how important they really are. They deal with pension investments and payments, land use, tax assessments, historic preservation, police conduct, public housing, libraries, recreation, and many other matters. It would be enlightening to choose one such board or commission in a city, township, or county and trace its history for a number of years. Who chose its members? How representative were they of the community's population? Why were they selected and what was the approval process? What were the board's powers? Did they derive from charter or state law? Was the board advisory? If so, how influential was it? Did it have decision-making authority? If so, could the local legislative body overturn its rulings? Did the board have a budget? If so, did funds come from the local legislative body or from its own taxing and spending authority? In what formal and informal ways did the board operate? What part did administrators, technical staff, and elected officials play in the board's business? How much say did the public have? What was the relationship between elected officials and the appointive board?

Appointed administrative officials are a second group of people who work in local government. These include city managers; budget directors; treasurers; attorneys; court administrators; and directors of police, fire, public works, parks and recreation, and other departments. The history of any or all would be worthwhile. No matter which position one studies, several trends stand out. First, as local government has grown, the number of administrative officials has risen. Second, administration has shifted from generalists to specialists. Third, formal education in public administration and business has replaced on-the-job training. Finally, administrators tend to move from place to place and to identify more with their profession than with any locality. How have these tendencies shaped who runs local government and to whom local government responds?

Perhaps the most prominent local administrative official in the United States is the city manager. Canadian cities have Chief Administrative Officers, with less power than city managers. Most U.S. municipalities, unless they are very large or small, have city managers. They are the chief administrative officers of municipal government, in charge of daily business at city hall. They hire, direct, and evaluate department heads and often have extensive personnel authority. City managers are hired by and serve at the pleasure of councils. Similarly, many counties have county administrators chosen by county commissioners. Early twentieth-century urban reformers seeking to professionalize local government invented city managers. Compiling individual or collective biographies of a town's city managers or analyzing how city managers function would make excellent local history endeavors.

For a biographical approach, look at the backgrounds of a particular community's city managers. Dayton, Ohio, the first large place with a city manager (1913), hired Cincinnati's municipal engineer, Henry Waite, a former mining and railroad engineer. In 1940, over three-fifths of the city managers responding to a questionnaire were ex-engineers. By the late twentieth century, however, managers often trained by taking academic public administration courses. What preparation and prior experience did chief administrators in a locality under study have? What collective profile emerges as to gender, race, social class, and political affiliation? Were the city managers similar to or different from the population as a whole? With what consequences? What career

Municipal department heads Ann Arbor, Michigan, confer in the mid-1960s, an era of formal clothes, smoking, and few women and racial minorities in city hall. *Guy C. Larcom Papers, Box 10, Bentley Historical Library, University of Michigan.*

patterns did your city managers have? Were they long-time residents or mobile professionals? What difference did this make?

Another fruitful way to study city managers is to describe and assess their role in local government. To do this, it may be best to examine the recent past, as sources will be more plentiful. City charters divide authority neatly, with elected councils setting policy and appointed managers administrating it. Did the system in question actually work this way? To what degree did ostensibly nonpolitical managers advocate policy choices? Did they engage in council or community politics to advance their policies or strengthen their job security? With what consequences? Meanwhile, did elected officials involve themselves in administration? How? Why? To fulfill constituent requests? To remedy administrative failures? Is there a distinction between administration and policy or politics? Were council-manager relations harmonious, conflicting, or inconsistent? What accounts for these patterns? Even when mangers and councils were personally cooperative and politically harmonious, their perspectives differed. Managers saw themselves as knowledgable professionals who could judge which streets to pave or employees to hire. They sometimes saw elected officials as ill-informed amateurs swayed by parochial or political motives. Elected officials, in turn, often regarded managers as professional gypsies with shallow knowledge of and commitment to the community. Moreover, politicians never forgot that managers did not have to stand for election; thus, they lacked the direct accountability that lay at the basis of representative government.

City, township, and county attorneys (sometimes called corporation counsels) are less likely to fill the spotlight than chief administrators, but they, too, are worth researching. Legal officials give advice, represent government in court, review contracts, and draft proposed ordinances. Litigation ranges from routine prosecution of ordinance violations to highly publicized personnel, environmental or civil liberties conflicts. Although often politically compatible with managers and elected officials, local government attorneys also need professional skill. Expertise conveys authority, since disregarding legal advice can be costly and embarrassing. Those who decide to study their city, township, or county's legal office might start by asking what does it do? How many and what kinds of court cases does it handle? With what results? What is its influence at city or township hall? Who are the attorneys? Why are they working for local government? What personal backgrounds and career paths does one find? Do public attorneys differ from those in private practice?

ॐ ॐ ॐ ॐ ॐ

PROFESSIONALIZING MUNICIPAL GOVERNMENT: NINETEENTH-CENTURY MUNICIPAL ENGINEERS

Historians Stanley Schultz and Clay McShane argue that municipal engineers transformed local government and changed late nineteenth-century cities. Engineers designed streets, bridges, and water and sewer systems. They also pioneered comprehensive city planning and urban redevelopment, such as Boston's Back Bay landfill. Moreover, Schultz and McShane show how engineers left their mark on government by modernizing it and expanding its duties. Engineers' large and complex projects brought expertise, long-term planning, centralized bureaucracy, and fiscal control systems to city and county government.

To describe a new urban "strategic elite," Schultz and McShane used late nineteenth-century books, government reports, and articles in journals ranging from *Public Health, Scientific American,* and *Popular Science Monthly* to *Engineering News, Journal of the Association of Engineering Societies,* and *Journal of the American Engineering Society.* They combined these primary sources with information from dissertations, articles, and historical books on public health and planning and on specific projects in Boston, New York, and Chicago. Schultz and McShane used brief case studies to document broad themes. Their work skillfully links the rise of municipal engineers to major changes in local government.

Source: Stanley K. Schultz and Clay McShane, "To Engineer the Metropolis: Sewers, Sanitation, and City Planning in Late-Nineteenth-Century America," *Journal of American History,* 65 (September, 1978), 389–411.

ॐ ॐ ॐ ॐ ॐ

Most employees at city or township hall or at the county building do the routine tasks of operating government and providing public services. They rarely appear in newspapers or on television, and historians tend to ignore them, too. But overlooking them represents missed opportunity. Public employees are a varied group. They include men and women, people of different races and ethnic origins, ardent partisans and political independents, unionized and non-union workers, and career and temporary employees. They likely fall into one of these categories: (a) academically trained professionals, like accountants, planners, and public health nurses; (b) workers with specialized on-the-job training, such as technicians, equipment operators, police officers, and firefighters; (c) clerical and secretarial office workers; and (d) laborers in streets, parks and public buildings. Over time, the number of local government employees has increased substantially. Meanwhile, the proportion in each category changed, as technology and educational requirements rose.

Telling the story of a community's public workers would be a valuable local history venture. Who were they? From what ethnic, racial, religious, and economic backgrounds did they come? How important were public jobs for ethnic and minority communities? Did government employees and their jobs differ from private sector workers and work? If so, how and why? Why did people decide to seek public employment? How did they obtain, keep, and advance in their jobs? What were their duties? How did their tasks change over time? What was the relationship between public workers and the community?

Unskilled laborers have always been an important segment of the public workforce. They collected garbage; built, cleaned, and repaired streets; maintained parks; cleaned buildings; and did other routine tasks. Numerous in the past, unskilled workers have fallen to technological and financial pressures. Passenger-activated elevators replaced those run by paid operators; street-sweeping machines succeeded men with brooms. Moreover, in recent years, governments cut labor costs by contracting with private firms to do the work of public employees. By the mid-1990s, contract workers handled half the waste collection and about two-fifths of public building maintenance and street repair jobs in the United States. What is the history of a city's unskilled public workers? Trace their numbers and duties over time. Has the community contracted services to private firms? If so, how and why did officials make the decision? Who took part in this debate and what did they say? What has contracting meant for government, public employees, and residents?

Meanwhile, as government grew, the ranks of clerical and secretarial workers expanded. They, too, ought to receive attention. What duties did clerical workers have? Who took these jobs? What educational, class, and ethnic backgrounds did they have? What were the attractions of public sector office employment for these people? What proportions of men and women held these jobs? What accounts for this? Many scholars argue that office work became feminized in the late nineteenth-century with the introduction of typewriters and other office machines. But historian Cindy Aron questions this assumption in her study of federal clerical workers.

The number of professional employees of local government has also increased over the past century. This trend stems from the increasing demands we have placed on government and from our fondness for technology and expertise. Although more likely to stay in one community than administrators, professionals also have strong occupational identities. Their educational credentials and knowledge of what people value, like clean water and public health, have given professionals prestige and power. Thus, residents who readily criticize elected officials usually defer to professionals clothed in the armor of expertise. Accordingly, professionals enjoyed more job security and work autonomy than other public employees. For example, historian Jon Teaford found that by the late nineteenth century, big-city public school teachers held their jobs as long as they wished, even without tenure or other formalized job security. One can apply this discussion to any community.

Viewing public employment through the lens of race, ethnicity, or gender can provide new insights. For example, a line of inquiry might

Looking Around City Hall 41

be the history of male and female workers in a municipal or county government. What jobs did each have? Why? Did cities and counties define some jobs as male and others as female? What was the basis of such decisions? Did officials restrict hiring married women? Did sexual harassment occur? If so, did it become a public issue? Why or why not? How did the duties, pay, and promotion for men and women compare? What changes occurred over time? Did change come from economic forces (like labor shortages), from laws and court rulings, or from individual leadership or group pressure? How did men and women working for local government view their employment? As jobs or careers? As permanent or temporary? Do answers to these questions differ from what one would find in the private sector?

The study of ethnicity is another way to reveal local history. Massive waves of immigration, first from Europe, more recently from East and South Asia, Latin America, and the Caribbean, have shaped Canada and the United States. How have these newcomers affected a particular community's government? Researchers can adapt the gender-linked questions above to investigate immigrants and public employment in a locality. City records, census lists, and city directories can help answer questions. For example, what was the ethnic composition of the town's public labor force at one or more points in the past? Did immigrants hold all sorts of public jobs or were they concentrated in just a few? How did specific ethnic groups differ from each other? Ethnic groups more often saw other nationalities as competitors rather than fellow newcomers with common problems.

Another approach is to document the importance of public employment to various ethnic groups. Urban historians say that jobs in government and politically connected private business helped newcomers gain economic security. These jobs, along with federal employment, offered steady work for people without much formal training or education. For instance, by the 1890s, Chicago Italians got city jobs in unskilled labor, building and maintaining streets, sewers, parks, and mass transit lines. After 1900, a few joined the police and fire departments and some became school teachers. Windy City Polish-Americans followed a similar path. At first, their city jobs were mainly as street laborers. By the 1920s and 1930s, though, Poles worked at the Board of Election Commissioners, Chicago Sanitary District, and in various county offices. These jobs meant more to immigrants than bread on the table. They also signaled to both natives and newcomers that immigrants, too, were part of the community.

Public employment has also been important for African Americans,

Police officers, Deering Street Station, Chicago, 1872. Police and fire departments employed many immigrants, but earlier arrivals often hired countrymen, forcing later-arriving groups to turn elsewhere for public employment. *Chicago Historical Society, Photo Files, ICHi-25743.*

who faced more discrimination than did immigrants. What was the number and proportion of blacks in a community at one or more points in the past? Sources mentioned above can help trace how many African Americans worked for a city or county and what jobs they had. What were their successes and achievements? What types of discrimination did they face in hiring, pay, and job placement? Did it come from hiring officials, from white workers, or from both? One can get help answering these questions through records of state and federal agencies which received complaints. Also, NAACP and Urban League papers document job bias claims. For instance, Branch Files in the NAACP Papers at the Library of Congress have abundant evidence about local communities. While cities often hired African Americans as laborers, they long resisted giving them other jobs, especially in police and fire departments. After all, people in such positions wore uniforms, a symbol of power. And police had guns and clubs and gave orders, while firemen lived together at station houses.

Whether the subject is women, European or Asian immigrants, Hispanics, or African Americans, historians should consider how members of each group secured jobs in local government. Did they use networks of family and friends to get work? How important was voting power? In many times and places, officials used jobs to reward and maintain political loyalty. Often population and voting strength go together, as we see with blacks and Hispanics in many U.S. cities today. Until the 1960s, racial segregation created some job opportunities for blacks. For example, separate schools for each race in the South and many parts of the North meant jobs for black teachers and principals. And cities placed a few black police and firemen in black neighborhoods without offending many whites. Since the 1960s, civil rights law and court rulings have enabled women and racial minorities to gain more jobs in government. What has occurred in one specific local government? Has it adopted affirmative action or hiring and promotion quotas? Why? With what results? In many places, such programs had the most impact where barriers against minority and female personnel had been highest, as in policing and fire fighting.

ॐ ॐ ॐ ॐ ॐ

AFRICAN AMERICAN SUCCESS IN LOCAL GOVERNMENT JOBS: CHICAGO IN THE 1930s

In the 1930s, University of Chicago political scientist Harold F. Gosnell disclosed an unusual story. Using the press, interviews, and census and government data, Gosnell demonstrated that unlike elsewhere, African Americans were well represented in local government in the Windy City. Although overconcentrated in menial labor, blacks had an equitable percentage of jobs as clerks, librarians, welfare workers, probation and truancy officers, deputy sheriffs, and deputy court bailiffs. In addition, there were about 300 African American teachers and 135 policemen. By 1931, African American attorneys held one-seventh of the professional posts in the city's legal department. A black man, Robert L. Taylor, Assistant Attorney for the Cook County Board of Election Commissioners, was the leading authority on Illinois election law.

What explains such success? Both major parties were strong and wanted blacks' votes. Moreover, the Republicans (whom most blacks favored) had competitive factions and close nomination contests. This gave African American voters strategic importance in both primary and general elections. Black Chicagoans also voted in large numbers and had skilled political leaders. They used their voting power to get patronage jobs. At the same time, they secured positions granted by clearly defined criteria, like civil service test scores.

Source: Harold F. Gosnell, *Negro Politicians: The Rise of Negro Politics in Chicago* (Chicago: University of Chicago Press, 1935).

ॐ ॐ ॐ ॐ ॐ

As Chicago illustrates, political patronage was one route to public employment. Under this arrangement, political loyalty determined who worked for government. If individuals campaigned successfully for a winning candidate, faction, or party, a job in local government could be their reward. To keep it, they had to work in future campaigns, perhaps turning out a certain number of votes in their precinct. They also had to donate money, sometimes a percentage of their salary, to their political organization. If their side lost, the winners fired them and hired loyalists. Defenders of patronage claimed it made government represent the people and respond to them. In addition, patronage kept political parties strong by supplying money and campaign help. And this made for good government, for unlike special interest groups, parties were broadly based and open to all. Did a specific city, township, or county have a patronage system? What positions did it cover? Did it actually work according to this model? Did it do what its defenders claimed? What were its faults? Did it persist or did this community abolish it? How and why?

In the late nineteenth century, reformers invented a different way to choose public employees. The civil service, or merit, system required applicants to take competitive examinations testing skills and knowledge. Those with highest scores became eligible for appointment. Authorities decided promotions the same way. Under civil service, government workers who survived a probationary period won job security. Officials could neither fire them for political reasons nor require them to be politically active. Civil service also had a hierarchy of clearly defined job grades, duties, and salaries. Advocates argued that civil service made government more efficient. Officials would no longer hire workers mainly for political rewards, and public employees would spend time on their jobs, not on campaigns. Above all, reformers claimed, government would hire the best qualified, not the politically well connected. Civil service, they hoped, would also reduce corruption and weaken political parties. Ironically, some party organizations backed civil service, too. They sometimes did so to win public approval and to give job security to people they had already hired.

An investigator can test these claims by examining evidence from a local community. Did the city or county adopt civil service? When and why? Did it bring the progress its advocates predicted? What problems did it have? How has the civil service system changed over time? What difference did it make in who got public jobs? Did civil service help applicants who did well on tests and hurt those who did not? What impact did this have? Did the merit system improve the quality of service to the public? Critics claim it made government less responsive, since workers with job security had little to fear from public opinion or from their poor job performance. How extensively did government implement civil service? Did it cover all jobs or exempt some? Did public officials evade civil service? Did they retain "temporary" positions for a long time? Did they give exams rarely? Or did they manipulate tests or corrupt the exam process? With what results? Even after civil service hiring, unfavored applicants could run into trouble. Supervisors could fire them during probationary periods or make things so unpleasant that they quit or requested transfers.

In the last forty years, labor unions have become prominent in federal, state, and local government. As unions in the private sector have withered or stagnated, the National Education Association (NEA), American Federation of Teachers (AFT), and the American Federation of State, County, and Municipal Employees (AFSCME) have grown and rank among the largest U.S. unions. In addition, teamsters (IBT), auto workers (UAW), and service employees (SEIU) have each organized large numbers of local government workers. Public employee unions are even stronger in Canada than in the United States.

The long history of public sector unions deserves attention. In the 1890s, New York City police and firemen formed organizations that gradually evolved from benevolent and lobbying associations into unions. Meanwhile, Margaret Haley organized the Chicago Teachers Federation, which helped start the American Federation of Teachers in 1916. The same era saw strikes by street sweepers and garbage collectors (New York, Trenton, Jersey City, and Providence, 1906–1913), police (Cincinnati and Boston, 1918–1919), and firemen. Wisconsin state employees launched AFSCME in 1932, which won its first major contract with Philadelphia in 1939.

In the 1960s and early 1970s, public employee unions grew enormously. Local government expanded greatly, especially in welfare, health, and education and hired many young, liberal human service providers. At the same time, U.S. cities and counties employed more low-paid workers (many of them African American or Hispanic) to clean buildings, collect garbage, and staff public hospitals. For these employees, the language and methods of the black civil rights movement became a model for union activism. State laws about public sector labor relations changed, too, in the 1960s and early 1970s. Many cities and states now recognized employees' rights to join unions, negotiate contracts, and even to strike. As a result, AFSCME contracts with local governments jumped from 400 in the early 1960s to 1,200 by 1971. At the same time, teachers, nurses, garbage collectors, police officers, firefighters, and welfare workers walked out on strike with increasing frequency.

It can be worthwhile to uncover the history of public employee unions and labor relations in a community. Does the city, township, or county have such unions? If not, why not? Did workers attempt to unionize? Why did these efforts fail? Examine laws, public opinion, and the behavior of public officials, workers, and unions to explain what happened. Union publications and archives, as well as local sources, may tell the story. If a local government has public employee unions, it should be possible to trace the history of one of them. Start at the beginning. What were the organizing issues? Who were the early union leaders? How did they differ from other workers? How did the union win its early contracts? What did the contracts say? Describe the collective bargaining process. Did strikes, lockouts, or any other job actions occur? What happened and what were the outcomes? How did labor-management relations evolve since collective bargaining began?

How do labor relations in government compare with those in the private sector? For one thing, the legal framework may well be different for each. What laws govern public-sector labor negotiations and strikes? Second, professional and clerical workers make up a large share of public employee unions. What difference does this make in the nature of labor unionism? Third, public opinion counts for more in public-sector labor relations than it does for private employers. Residents pay taxes to and have more control over local government. Also, strikes by police officers, teachers, or garbage collectors disrupt daily life more than most private-sector strikes. Therefore, people can be more hostile toward strikes by government workers and toward demands that may increase taxes.

But the public and private sectors are similar in important ways. Collective bargaining and contract administration are much alike in each. Furthermore, in recent years, local governments and corporations both faced financial pressure. Thus, cities and counties have implemented speed-ups, wage squeezes, and layoffs just as have private employers. In fact, the trend toward privatizing public services reflects not only conservative ideology but public officials' need to limit spending.

In comparing public employee and private-sector unions, there are several things to consider. Both bargain for and administer contracts and handle grievances and arbitration hearings. But in local government, typically several unions deal with each city, township, or county. By contrast, often big national or multinational corporations face only one union. Next, some public sector unions are also occupational associations, concerned about training and professional standards. Third, while both private and public-sector unions are politically active, the latter tend to be more intensely involved in local politics. Government workers' unions lobby city councils and county boards for better pay and conditions. In many places, public workers live where they work, forming an important voting bloc. Governments used to restrict employees' political activity to curb coercion of workers by elected officials. These restrictions have waned, however. Public employees are often heavily involved in local elections with union endorsements, financial contributions, and campaign volunteers. Is this the case in the community being studied? How successful are these unions in getting what they want?

This chapter introduced some historical elements of cities, townships, and counties. It called attention to various types of local government. The chapter also offered a chance to think about relations among local governments and between local and state and federal government. Next, it encouraged readers to notice the physical presence of government through its buildings and impact on landscapes and streetscapes. Finally, it emphasized the importance of public employees. The variety of government jobs, the backgrounds of public workers, and public-sector personnel issues each are part of this mix. Perhaps one or more of the topics in this chapter can become the focus for a project in local history. On the other hand, researchers can also use these ideas and information as background to do the history of a government function, like police, fire, or parks. It is to those areas that we turn in Chapter 4.

SUGGESTED READINGS

Jon Teaford tells the story of twentieth-century suburban government and politics in *Post-Suburbia: Government and Politics in the Edge Cities* (Baltimore: Johns Hopkins University Press, 1997). Teaford discusses city-suburban consolidation in *City and Suburb: The Political Fragmentation of Metropolitan America, 1850–1970* (Baltimore: Johns Hopkins University Press, 1979). David Rusk, who has local, state, and federal government experience, argues for metropolitan coordination in *Cities Without Suburbs* (Washington, DC: Woodrow Wilson Center Press, 1993).

The standard history of urban-federal relations is Mark Gelfand's *A Nation of Cities: The Federal Government and Urban America, 1933–1965* (New York: Oxford University Press, 1975). Gelfand describes a steadily growing federal commitment to cities, culminating in the creation of the Department of Housing and Urban Development in 1965. But a study of urban-federal relations since then might reach a different conclusion. Work on federal-city relations in the 1930s includes Charles H. Trout, *Boston: The Great Depression and the New Deal* (New York: Oxford University Press, 1977); Jo Ann E. Argersinger, *Toward a New Deal in Baltimore: People and Government in the Great Depression* (Chapel Hill: University of North Carolina Press, 1988); and Douglas L. Smith, *The New Deal in the Urban South* (Baton Rouge: Louisiana State University Press, 1988). Philip J. Funigiello, *The Challenge to Urban Liberalism: Federal-City Relations during World War II* (Knoxville: University of Tennessee Press, 1978), emphasizes housing and planning.

Two collections of essays and articles on urban redevelopment are Jewel Bellush and Murray Hausknecht, eds., *Urban Renewal: People, Politics and Planning* (Garden City, NY: Doubleday, 1967), and James Q. Wilson, ed., *Urban Renewal: The Record and the Controversy* (Cambridge: Massachusetts Institute of Technology Press, 1966). Teaford, *The Rough Road to Renaissance: Urban Revitalization in America, 1940–1985* (Baltimore: Johns Hopkins University Press, 1990), is a comprehensive treatment emphasizing large northeastern and midwestern cities. William L. Lebovich, *America's City Halls* (Washington, DC: Preservation Press, 1984), illustrates 114 structures from the Historic American Buildings Survey.

Jon C. Teaford, *The Unheralded Triumph: City Government in America, 1870–1900* (Baltimore: Johns Hopkins University Press, 1984), argues that big city government functioned successfully and stresses the growing importance of professionals and experts. The history of gender and public employment still awaits attention. For ethnicity and public employment, see Humbert S. Nelli, *The Italians in Chicago, 1880–1930: A Study in Ethnic Mobility* (New York: Oxford University Press, 1970); Edward R. Kantowicz, *Polish-American Politics in Chicago, 1888–1940* (Chicago: University of Chicago Press, 1975); and Stephen P. Erie, *Rainbow's End: Irish-Americans and the Dilemmas of Urban Ma-*

chine Politics, 1840–1985 (Berkeley: University of California Press, 1988). For black public employees, consult books on African Americans in specific cities. Examples include Howard N. Rabinowitz, *Race Relations in the Urban South, 1865–1890* (Urbana: University of Illinois Press, 1980); George C. Wright, *Life Behind a Veil: Blacks in Louisville, Kentucky, 1865–1930* (Baton Rouge: Louisiana State University Press, 1985); Richard W. Thomas, *Life for Us Is What We Make It: Building Black Community in Detroit, 1915–1945* (Bloomington: Indiana University Press, 1992); and Kenneth L. Kusmer, *A Ghetto Takes Shape: Black Cleveland, 1870–1930* (Urbana: University of Illinois Press, 1976). Each also covers black political activity. The portrait of federal clerical workers in Cindy Sondik Aron's *Ladies and Gentlemen of the Civil Service: Middle-Class Workers in Victorian America* (New York: Oxford University Press, 1987) offers a model for research on local government employees. Two samples of work on urban public sector unions are Sterling D. Spero and John M. Capozzola, *The Urban Community and Its Unionized Bureaucracies: Pressure Politics in Local Government Labor Relations* (New York: Dunellen, 1973), and Mark H. Maier, *City Unions: Managing Discontent in New York City* (New Brunswick, NJ: Rutgers University Press, 1987). See also Robert H. Connery and William V. Farr, eds., *Unionization of Municipal Employees, Proceedings of The Academy of Political Science* (v. 30, n. 2; New York: Columbia University Press, 1970).

Chapter 4

PROBING THE HISTORY OF LOCAL GOVERNMENT SERVICES

Most contact with local government comes through the services it provides. Cities, townships, and counties fight crime and fires, maintain streets, furnish water, dispose of garbage and sewage, operate recreation facilities and programs, and do scores of other things. Each has rich potential for work in local history. This chapter will describe what local governments do, suggest questions to ask, and provide guidance to sources. Besides focusing on a government service itself, researchers can use it to show how citizens have thought about what government should do and why. Thus, historians not only chronicle the past but also speak to the present.

No matter which local service they study, good historians start by asking why it became a government responsibility. What did people want government to do? Why? Why didn't they leave a task to individuals, business, or private nonprofit agencies? Was there consensus or conflict about the scope of government? How have public responsibilities changed over time? Which duties did people give to cities or counties, and which did they assign to states or provinces or to national government? Current political arguments about the size of the public sector show that these issues are rarely settled.

Once people decide to give local government responsibility for a particular service, they make other decisions that are interesting to study. How should the city or township fulfill its duties? Garbage collection and disposal provides a good example. Did local government act directly, hiring workers, buying trucks, and running a landfill? Or did it pay another government, such as the county or a larger city, to take care of its trash? Perhaps a town combined with others in a regional service agency. Or maybe it bought garbage services from a private business. If so, from one or several? If the latter, did businesses compete or did each have exclusive rights to a certain area? In making such decisions, legal, political, financial, and technical factors all came into play. What alternatives did officials consider? How much did each option cost? How important was cost? Which option served residents equally? Was most responsive to residents? A narrative and analysis of how a community defined a government function would make a fascinating public history project.

Consider, too, how a local government distributed a particular service. Did all benefit equally or did some get better treatment than others? Did inequities one finds stem from politics, geography, social class, or race? For instance, historian Olivier Zunz found that a century ago in Detroit, newly developed outlying residential areas had modern water pipes, sewers, and paved streets, but the working-class east side did not. In *Down from Equality: Black Chicagoans and the Public Schools, 1920–1941,* I disclosed that by the late 1930s, the Board of Education in the Windy City spent less per capita on black children than on either upper-status whites or European immigrants. Moreover, school overcrowding occurred almost exclusively in the black ghetto. Exploring the question of equity for any public service in any locality is engrossing.

Finally, it can be enlightening to uncover fiscal aspects of a community's service decisions. How much did it spend on any specific function? How did that amount compare to other parts of the budget? How much service did the money buy? Did allocated funds meet public demand? How can one determine this? Next, how did the community pay for the service in question? Did funds come from current general revenue, bonds, special assessments, or users' fees? Why did local officials choose a particular financing method? What were its consequences? Did some pay more than the benefits they received? Did others pay less?

Suppose a city funded street paving from current revenue. In that case, residents paid on the basis of their property tax bills, not according to how much they used the streets. Meanwhile, under-assessed, tax-abated, or tax-exempt property owners (such as churches, schools, and most hospitals) underpaid or paid nothing for smooth streets. As another example, some large cities enacted municipal income taxes, which both shifted the tax burden within their boundaries and forced nonresidents employed in that city to help pay for city government. Nonresidents who shopped or played in a city but did not work there, however, escaped that cost unless that city had a municipal sales tax. If the state helped fund local governments, though, all its taxpayers paid a little to each city.

Each method of financing municipal services has its own consequences. Did a city pay for street paving with long-term bonds? If so, future residents would help fund past construction. Did officials finance streets, sidewalks, and sewers through special tax assessments on just some property? If so, a few pay for improvements that benefit all. Roger Simon found that when Milwaukee did this a hundred years ago, many working-class homeowners rejected such amenities owing to their cost. Accordingly, their neighborhoods were less pleasant and their death rates higher. User fees are yet another way to pay for public services. Such fees have political appeal, since they fall on those who benefit, often at the time of service. Although public swimming pools can charge admission, doing so can exclude low-income residents. Moreover, it may be impractical to finance street lights or sewers on the basis of usage. Researchers can look into the history of user fees in a community and assess their results.

When beginning to investigate the history of a local public service, researchers should consult the guide to sources in Chapter 2. In addition, they will want to locate primary sources appropriate for each particular topic. For example, where are the records that document the number, type, and disposition of calls for police service at various times in the past? Other historians, meanwhile, will match data in county property tax files with real estate sales data to uncover assessment practices. In addition to public records, they may use journals, newsletters, and archives of professional organizations to trace the history of local public works, planning, or fire fighting, to name a few. It is wise to include physical evidence as well. Do sidewalks display the year of construction? If so, how does the date compare with the year adjacent buildings were erected? What does the answer reveal about neighborhood history?

Among local government services, policing is the most expensive and controversial. Police, crime, and public order are fertile areas for local historians. Police can deny people their freedom and use physical, even deadly, force. What have these powers meant in your community's history?

One worthwhile line of inquiry concerns police officers themselves. Who worked for the city police or county sheriff's department? What were their social backgrounds? In many places, most police were young, white, working-class or lower-middle-class men. Women, members of racial minorities, and the affluent were rare on police forces. How did these class, gender, and racial patterns shape police-citizen relations? Police reactions to racial and political protest? Why did police officers choose their line of work? How did they get their jobs? Did they value job security or upward mobility? Did they

Probing the History of Local Government Services 53

Detroit police, 1939. What does this photograph of police in the late 1930s convey? How would different observers have answered this question? *Charles W. Ungermann Papers, Box 1, Bentley Historical Library, University of Michigan.*

stay in the same place or move from one community to another? Did these patterns change over time? Finally, a local historian can look into the inner world of police. How did they view their job responsibilities? Relations with residents? With elected officials and administrators? How did they spend their leisure time? With whom did they socialize?

Another path of historical research leads to what a community expected from law enforcement agencies. Should police prevent crime or catch lawbreakers? If the latter, did this include motorists violating traffic rules? Did a city want its police to keep order? If so, did this mean defending the powerful by protecting their property, scattering loiterers, and suppressing disorderly workers, students, or blacks? Or did a community instruct its police to defend Bill of Rights freedoms, even when dissenters sought social change? Were the police supposed to aid the needy? Nineteenth-century police sheltered the homeless and cared for lost children. Did residents and

Detroit police removing striker, 1937. Whose police? Employers and striking workers did not agree. *Library of Congress, LC-USZ62–106935-DLC.*

insurers want police to take reports of accidents, robberies, and burglaries? Or did the town want its police to regulate public behavior? Private behavior? At various times, lawmakers told police to suppress prostitution, gambling, liquor sales and drinking, homosexual relations, boxing matches, and Sabbath-breaking. How did a particular community decide what it wanted its police to do? Did consensus prevail? If not, what conflicts erupted? Did a city give its police contradictory or inconsistent instructions? If so, what problems did this cause for police in their contacts with residents? For example, what happened when working-class police got orders to attack strikers? When officials told police to enforce moral codes neither they nor many residents accepted? On the one hand, police made money protecting illegal pastimes. When one nineteenth-century New York City police captain won a transfer to a red-light district, he rejoiced that his diet changed "from salt chuck to tenderloin." But when law enforcers became lawbreakers, they and their departments lost public respect.

In considering what a city expected of its police, researchers enter the thicket of police-community relations. Each task officials gave police required different kinds of contacts with residents. Service called for one type of police behavior; enforcing morality or suppressing dissent called for another. Moreover, "police-community relations" ignores the existence of many communities, not just one. Under what circumstances did police meet well-off residents? How did police deal with them? If police were deferential and helpful, upper-status residents regarded police favorably. How did police act in immigrant, minority, and working-class neighborhoods? What explains the answers? Police officers' own racial and ethnic opinions? Attitudes of police commanders? Of influential people in the community? The greater violence and crime in these districts? How did your police treat crime in minority, immigrant, and working-class neighborhoods? Resentment against police harassment, violence, and negligence sparked rioting in U.S. cities from the 1960s to the 1990s. Have police-community relations in your area reflected national patterns? Have they differed? How and why?

If the entire topic of police-community relations is too vast, historians can select a single segment. Here are three examples. Did a community establish a citizens' advisory committee or police review board? Why or why not? If so, what did it do? How did police administrators, officers, and residents react to it? A second field of study is the history of female, African American, Asian, or Hispanic police officers in a locality. How many were there? Who were they? When and why did they join the force? What were their experiences within the department? How did their gender or racial identity affect their jobs as police officers? Did the department adopt affirmative action guidelines for hiring and promotion? With what results? Community policing is a third possible area. What is the history of beat policing (assigning officers to specific territories) in a given city? Of foot, bicycle, or vehicle patrols? How did various neighborhood groups interact with police or sheriff's deputies? What is the history of neighborhood watch or crime watch groups in an area? Did police welcome or resent citizen involvement? Did officers want supervisors to assign them to civilian-police crime prevention, or did they dismiss it as not "real" police work?

One approach to police history is to describe and explain how a department changed over time. How much policing did the community want? Those desiring small and cheap government, feeling unmenaced by crime, or fearing that police threatened liberty wanted minimal policing. But persons who believed that crime and public disorder were excessive favored more police with more authority. This view spread in the 1840s and 1850s, when several major U.S. cities created uniformed, full-time, salaried police forces organized hierarchically under military-style discipline. Such departments soon became a standard of urban life, a way for cities to show how modern they were.

Each community also had to decide how close police should be to electoral politics. In nineteenth-century U.S. cities, police hiring, transfer, and promotion decisions were political, and police paid politicians to get and keep their jobs. When an incumbent party or faction lost, the winners could hire new policemen. In the twentieth century, this arrangement slowly faded, and police departments became more professionalized, bureaucratic, and centralized. Competitive exams determined hiring and promotion. Police had more schooling and formal training. Written procedures governed job routines. Describe a particular city's experience. What were the advantages and disadvantages of each of these systems? Which was more responsive to the public? Which offered better service?

Technology is another part of police history. By the end of the nineteenth century, police called precinct stations from street-corner boxes and used photograph files to identify suspects. In the twentieth century, fingerprinting, crime labs, and computers each altered police work. One can probe the arrival and impact of a new police technology in a community. Why did officials adopt the new method? Did the department resist or welcome it? How did new technology change police behavior? The answers can be complex. For example, automobiles took police from walking beats to patrol cars. This meant that more police-citizen contacts occurred in times of crisis, and this changed relations with civilians. Autos also meant police officers were directing traffic and enforcing parking and traffic laws. Since many motorists violated these regulations from time to time, police apprehended well-dressed, affluent people more than before. Since police could not catch everyone who broke traffic rules, upper-status people learned police could be unfair, something the less fortunate had long known.

Local historians interested in the law may gravitate toward legal aspects of police work. How did city police or county sheriff's deputies balance individual rights with effective crime control? Did police perceive a conflict between the two? What did police do after they apprehended criminal suspects? Did police behavior change following U.S. Supreme Court rulings in the 1960s requiring them to inform suspects of their rights, permit legal counsel, and abstain from using illegally seized evidence? If so, how and with what results? Did local police or county sheriff departments spy on civilians? If so, who were the targets and what did police do? What happened to the information they collected? Did victims of spying challenge police behavior? With what outcome?

As noted, police have been lawbreakers as well as law enforcers. In *The Police and the Public* (New Haven, CT: Yale University Press, 1971), sociologist Albert Reiss reported that one-fifth of the police who knew a survey team was observing them violated the law, usually by accepting money, meals, or other gifts from civilians in exchange for favors. What is the history of police crime in a community? Did police accept bribes or payoffs to ignore or protect illegal activity? Did they take money from legal businesses or law-abiding individuals for good will or extra service? Did they steal money or goods held as evidence? Did they take part in or condone drug dealing, burglary, and other criminal activity? Did police assault or kill civilians? How much illegal police conduct became public? How was it revealed? How did police administrators, elected officials, the press, and the public respond? What were the results for police and for elected officials?

Finally, it can be instructive to find out how localities dealt with crime. Although U.S. state and Canadian national and provincial government defined most crimes, cities and townships also enacted ordinances with civil and criminal penalties. How did your locality define crime? Did its definition change over time? If so, how and why? How much crime actually existed in a city or county at various times in the past? How useful are crime statistics in answering this question? What did a specific community tell its police to do about crime? Since police did not control most causes of crime, they might find it impossible to meet public expectations. Did the community tell police to keep order? In that case, arrests for drunk and disorderly conduct, loitering, and vagrancy would abound, and crime rates would be high. Or did residents want police to prioritize crimes against people? Which people? Against property? What do local crime statistics reveal? What conclusions can one draw from the class, race, or ethnicity of perpetrators? Of victims? Was crime a political issue in your community? As these questions demonstrate, crime is significant and complex and thus well-suited for local historians.

Ordinance enforcement is a specialized type of policing that municipalities and townships did. Local governments enacted many regulations to protect community health, safety, and appearance. Such rules required residents to cut grass and weeds, clear sidewalks of snow, keep vehicles off lawns, prevent accumulation of junk, and place garbage at curbside only at certain times and days. Ordinance enforcement was rarely newsworthy. However, it could stir strong feelings among ordinance violators and their neighbors who sometimes feuded over annoyances such as abandoned automobiles and untrimmed hedges obstructing sidewalks.

Uncovering the history of ordinance enforcement in a community can make a worthy local history project. One can trace the legislative history of such ordinances. A second task is to describe enforcement administration and procedures in a city or township. Third, researchers can analyze patterns of enforcement. What ordinances did officials take seriously and which did they neglect? Did enforcement vary from one part of the community to another? Which rules did citizens obey and which did they resist? Department files, court records, and interviews can provide some answers.

Historians by and large have neglected the story of municipal and county courts. How did a city or county organize its courts? Did this structure change over time? If so, how and why? What explains the creation of specialized courts such as juvenile and probate? Who served as local judges? How were they chosen? What was their relationship with the community? Who else worked for the courts and what did they do? What kinds of cases came before the courts? Did this change? How and why? Under what circumstances did judges or juries decide cases? When and how often did out of court settlements take place? What is the history of plea bargaining? What patterns can one detect in the result of court cases? Who served on juries? Who was excluded? How did news media and the public view the courts? One can pursue these issues through court records which normally are available to the public. Judges do, however, sometimes seal cases (and this is itself worthy of study). In addition, it is useful to interview court employees and draw upon newspaper accounts.

Preventing and extinguishing fires, another major local government service, often cost cities and townships more than anything other than police. The many questions to ask about police also apply to firefighters and fire departments. These include the backgrounds and careers of firefighters, job duties, work culture, and community relations. New technology, like horse-drawn and motorized vehicles, alarm boxes and radios, protective gear, ladders, chemical foam, and smoke detectors, changed fire fighting in important ways. Tracing the chronological development of a local fire department can be interest-

Probing the History of Local Government Services 59

City firemen on truck, Ypsilanti, Michigan, 1929–1930. As technology became costly and complex, more communities shifted from volunteer to professional fire fighting forces. Competition with other localities was another reason to create full-time, salaried departments. *Ypsilanti Historical Archives.*

ing. Did the community begin with a volunteer fire company? Small towns usually had one. Large cities had several or many volunteer fire companies, organized along ethnic, political, or neighborhood lines. Members enjoyed socializing at their clubhouse, brawling with rival companies, and racing to fires.

Privately sponsored volunteer forces rarely survived the mid-nineteenth-century. Did a locality retain the volunteer system but bring it under government control? If so, when and why? Or did the city or township replace volunteers with full-time, salaried, uniformed employees? Describe how and why this occurred.

As governments created fire departments, they built structures to house them. One can study a community's fire stations. What architectural styles appeared? Are they ornate or functional? How large are the buildings? Did people use them for other purposes, too? Compare fire stations from different times to trace how and why they have changed.

Just as police professionalized in the twentieth century, so did fire departments, and one can explore that process. At what point did a city use physical and written examinations for hiring and promotion? Did it step up formal training and adopt standards from national associations? Perhaps a locality also increased firefighters' duties. Fire prevention may have been one. Did the fire department tell residents what caused fires and how to prevent them? Did the city or township enact building codes and inspect buildings to curb fire losses? Who devised fire suppression standards? What department enforced them? Officials also ordered fire departments to respond to medical emergencies and rescue calls. How well did firefighters do this? Did the fire department also have other assignments as well? By the 1980s and 1990s, some

Late 19th-century volunteer firemen, Ypsilanti, Michigan. Firefighters' male work culture bears investigation. How did work routines create powerful bonds? What was the role of physical danger? The importance of obtaining and caring for equipment? Unlike most other workers, firemen on extended duty shifts ate, slept, and spent leisure time with coworkers. Did your fire department celebrate new hires, new equipment, and retirements with special ceremonies? Did firefighters show off their vehicles, equipment, and uniforms in parades? Did they stage firefighting exhibitions and contests of skill? Have such customs changed or stayed the same in a particular locality? *Ypsilanti Historical Archives.*

communities tried to save money by combining fire and police dispatching or even by merging separate police and fire units into combined public safety departments. Did this occur in the area under study? With what advantages and disadvantages?

Finally, it is interesting to compare public opinion toward police and firefighters. Late-nineteenth-century popular music, melodrama, and lithographs portrayed firemen as heroes. Why? What was similar about the job duties of police and firefighters? What was different? How was each group separate from the public? What did each do to promote its image in the community?

A third thing local government does is pave, repair, and clean streets. If this is of interest, the historian can start at the beginning. Who laid out town or county streets and roads? Local government? Private land developers? Did streets predate local government? Besides standard streets, does an area have boulevards, roadways sandwiched around a small park-like strip of grass and trees? Does your city have limited-access expressways? When were they built? Why? How were they financed? Who determined their locations? What were the results for traffic and for adjacent land? Observe street patterns. Are blocks long or short? Are streets narrow as in downtown Boston or wide like those in Salt Lake City? What explains these choices? Are there grid patterns? Diagonal spokes from a center hub? Curving, winding streets? What do each of these patterns say? Does your area have dead-end streets or cul de sacs? Why? Are local streets the product of a unified plan? Many separate plans? No plans? Each arrangement reveals beliefs of those who shaped their environment.

Another set of questions to ask about a community's streets concerns their purposes. In an age of motor vehicles, we commonly regard streets as exclusively for traffic. But this has not been true in the past, nor is it always so today. What uses have a town's residents made of their streets? Visiting and exchanging information? Playing games? Selling things? Holding community events, like parades, art fairs, street festivals, and neighborhood block parties? Expressing opinions about candidates, strikes, wars, and racial injustice?

Who controlled local streets? How did they exert this power? What conflicts arose over use of streets, and how were these disputes settled? In *Parades and Power: Street Theatre in Nineteenth-Century Philadelphia* (Philadelphia: Temple University Press, 1986), historian Susan G. Davis described struggles between rich and poor over recreation, political rallies, and vending in streets and public squares. Meanwhile, after the Pennsylvania legislature authorized a railroad to lay track in the street of one Philadelphia neighborhood, residents stoned con-

Commercial streetscape, North West 13th Street, Gainesville, Florida, 1996. In the twentieth century, motor vehicles captured and transformed streets. What part did local government play in this change? *Photo by author.*

struction crews and destroyed track until officials backed down. Competition over public space continues in our time. From early twentieth-century St. Louis to South Florida, San Antonio, and California today, local government has permitted developers or property owners to privatize formerly public space by erecting fences and gates to exclude outsiders. Communities such as Miami Shores, Florida, barricade public streets to turn away nonresidents. Elsewhere, Toronto, Chicago, and Washington, D.C., enacted permit systems to ban nonresident parking in congested neighborhoods. What struggles over public streets have occurred in your community? How were they fought?

Street paving is another topic for local historians. Here, too, they face issues of money, technology, social values, and equity. When were local streets paved? Why? Did officials pave streets to move goods more easily? To make travel more pleasant? To show how modern the city was? What paving materials did your local government use? How did it decide? Before the Civil War, wood blocks or cobblestones on sand foundations were popular. Later, officials turned to

Probing the History of Local Government Services 63

Street paving crew, Ypsilanti, Michigan, n.d. As cities grew, street paving generated jobs for laborers and contracts for construction firms. *Ypsilanti Historical Archives.*

gravel, macadam (crushed stone), and brick or granite blocks. In the twentieth century, asphalt and concrete paving prevailed, for they offered smooth, durable surfaces.

Students of local paving may wish to examine how authorities made decisions. Did they pave streets when neighborhoods were first settled? Did all parts of the community get paved streets? What patterns exist? Who decided to pave a street—city council or township board, individual elected officials, or nonelected staff? What criteria did they use? Did the public want streets paved? Why or why not? Who paid? Did government use special assessments or general revenues? Current operating funds or bonds? Who did the paving? Public employees or privately owned construction firms? If the latter, how did officials select them? Did government regulate who contractors hired or how they did their job? Similar questions apply to histories of street repair and resurfacing.

Lighting is another facet of the streetscape local government often controls. One would want to begin by adapting questions about finance, technology, public opinion, and distribution patterns listed

Street cleaning, St. Louis, ca. 1906. Historians of street cleaning address changing technology, equity of service, and finances. How often did a city clean local streets? What methods did officials use? Were some streets cleaned more than others? If so, why? For many places, snow removal is worthy of study, too. What methods did local governments use? Who decided? Was there dispute about snow removal? *National Archives, Record Group 21, U.S. District Court, Eastern District of Missouri, NRE 21-EMOSTLE&L-E&L9028-STLCC37.*

above. Did street lighting have symbolic as well as practical meanings? For example, did it suggest residents' acceptance of the change from farm to city life? Did it reflect embrace of modernity and progress? In many communities, street lights were a partnership between local government and investor-owned private utilities. Look into this relationship. Who decided to install or upgrade lights? What political and financial pressures influenced these decisions? To trace this story, utility archives and publications can supplement government records.

A third part of the streetscape is urban forestry. In many communities, local government plants, trims, removes, and replaces trees that line streets. Besides exploring decision making, finance, and equity, one can ask who did urban forestry work? What were their qualifications? What were the functional and aesthetic dimensions of the appeal of tree-lined streets to public officials and residents? What cultural statements did urban trees make? Besides research in public

Bridge over Huron River, Michigan Avenue, Ypsilanti, Michigan, 1869. The history of a bridge can attract local historians. Who authorized and paid for it? Why? Who designed it? What was its design and technology? What difference did it make for the community's economy and land use? Did it help develop empty or sparsely occupied land? Did it lead to a new local government or to the merger of previously separate towns? *Ypsilanti Historical Archives.*

records, one should find out how well different species of trees survive under urban conditions.

Alleys, passages splitting blocks at the back of lot lines, are part of streetscapes in some cities. They, too, offer opportunities for local historians. Did a city have alleys? What were their uses for homeowners? For businesses? What nontraffic functions did alleys serve for adults and for children? What happened to alleys in the twentieth century? Explain the change. Note the decline of home deliveries by business. Observe, too, architectural fashion merging garages into homes and placing them facing the front of residential lots.

Parks are another major responsibility of local government. The most direct forerunners of urban parks were nineteenth-century landscaped cemeteries, whose curved paths, natural foliage, and monuments drew weekend pleasure-seekers. Building on these attractions, pioneer park designers hoped natural parks would improve the physical and spiritual health of residents of crowded cities. They designed parks for calm leisure, like walks and picnics, not for active play. Businessmen and politicians backed parks for the prestige and prosperity they would bring. Politicians also liked park projects for the jobs and profitable land and construction contracts they created. Real estate developers believed new parks would accelerate nearby settlement and raise property values. What individuals and groups led local parks efforts? What were their arguments? Did they have other motives they did not publicly articulate? Did some oppose establishing parks? If so, who and why?

༃༃༃༃༃

A MODEL FOR URBAN PARKS: NEW YORK CITY'S CENTRAL PARK

Though not the first, New York City's Central Park shaped the city park movement. Calvert Vaux and Frederick Law Olmsted won a design competition in the late 1850s with a plan that created, in landscape historian David Schuyler's words, "the country within the city." It did this with winding lanes, broad lawn vistas, and many shrubs and trees. Vaux and Olmsted put roads crossing the park below grade level and planted trees at the park's borders to separate it from the city beyond. They also clustered required buildings at the edge to keep most of the park natural. While Vaux and Olmsted emphasized nature, Central Park was, of course, contrived and arranged. The designers transformed a partly swampy dump, sprinkled with squatters' shanties, into a symbol of natural tranquility. Other cities quickly followed. Philadelphia enlarged Fairmont Park, Baltimore created Druid Hill Park, and Brooklyn built Prospect Park. By the late 1800s, some cities moved from individual showcase parks to large park systems. Vaux and Olmsted designed one for Buffalo linked by tree-lined boulevards. They also planned Chicago's South Park System anchored by Jackson and Washington Parks. But it was Central Park that set the standard in park design for America's cities.

Sources: Roy Rosenzweig and Elizabeth Blackmar, *The Park and the People: A History of Central Park* (Ithaca, NY: Cornell University Press, 1992); and David Schuyler, *The New Urban Landscape: The Redefinition of City Form in Nineteenth-Century America* (Baltimore: Johns Hopkins University Press, 1986).

༃༃༃༃༃

Probing the History of Local Government Services 67

Carriages in Central Park, New York City, 1905. *Library of Congress,* LCD401–9285-DLC.

There is much to ponder in community park design. Who were the landscape architects? Were they local or not? How were they selected? What did their park designs try to achieve? From where did their ideas come? Did officials change park plans over the years? If so, how? Were parks individually developed or part of a centrally-planned system? Next, consider park locations. Who chose new park sites? What influenced those choices? What evidence remains about the land acquisition process? What information is available about constructing parks? Who did the labor? What technical, financial, and political issues arose during park construction? Finally, which local governments built and operated parks? While municipalities led the way, in recent decades, counties and special purpose districts have created park systems. Has this occurred in the area being investigated?

Historians are also interested in who used parks. Did they attract the wealthy, the middle class, or the masses? Newcomers or long-time residents? Mothers with children? Entire families? Single young men? Did the answer to this question vary among parks or within the same park? Did it change over time? Park use may have differed by social class, race and ethnicity, age, and gender. How did people use parks? For quiet contemplation or active play? If the latter, was it organized or informal? Did small or big groups socialize in parks? Were parks public spaces for large-scale entertainment like concerts? For political expression, either dissenting or supporting the social order? What clashes occurred among park users? Were conflicts based on differing activities? On race, class, gender, or age? How has the recent surge in physical exercise altered park usage?

Another question to ask is who controlled the parks. Local governments often regulate public parks by requiring permits for some gatherings, banning alcoholic beverages and certain sports, and closing parks at night. Did the selected community do this? Did it enforce these rules? What assumptions did such regulations reflect? What conflicts did they reveal? Did users themselves control the parks? If so, how? How did residents view the parks? As places of civic unity where

Children using play equipment in park, Price, Utah, 1946. Active play by young people is one among many park uses. *National Archives, Record Group 245, Coal Mines Administration, NWDNS-245-MS-534L.*

different people mixed? As turf contested by competing groups? As boundaries separating these groups? As sites for leisure-time fun? Or as dangerous, crime-infested jungles? As these questions suggest, park history is a window on a community as a whole.

༄༅༄༅༄༅༄༅༄༅

CONTESTED PARKS: THE CASE OF WORCESTER, MASSACHUSETTS

Some historians view urban parks as the work of upper-class reformers either creating spaces for their own leisure or trying to uplift the working class by exposing them to nature. Focusing on one New England city, historian Roy Rosenzweig drew a more complex picture.

Late nineteenth-century Worcester, Massachusetts, like many industrial towns of its day, was split between Irish Catholic workers and a Yankee Protestant elite. The latter, which included parks commissioner Edward Winslow Lincoln, felt parks should be peaceful, quiet, and orderly. Elm Park, on Worcester's comfortable west side, followed the Olmsted formula, with trees, shrubs, ponds, and bridges. But Worcester provided no recreational facilities for the densely-settled working-class east side.

In 1884, elite leaders proposed a new water reservoir to improve west side fire protection. Irish politicians blocked this plan until the board of aldermen approved east side playgrounds for active play. Even though these facilities would be crowded and underfunded, Worcester's immigrants had secured some park funds for themselves. Just as significant, they also defined their public places as they wished, using them for drinking, ethnic picnics, and sports and games. Rosenzweig drew on parks commission reports and minutes, petitions to city council, newspaper accounts, and theses and dissertations at Worcester's Clark University to enrich urban park history.

Source: Roy Rosenzweig, *Eight Hours For What We Will: Workers and Leisure in an Industrial City, 1870–1920* (Cambridge: Cambridge University Press, 1983).

༄༅༄༅༄༅༄༅༄༅

Soon after creating parks, local governments began public recreation programs. Several large eastern cities set up play sites for children in the 1880s and 1890s. By World War I, 480 U.S. cities had nearly four thousand playgrounds. Most accounts of the playground movement credit upper-status progressive reformers, who believed what

Elm Park, Worcester, Massachusetts, ca. 1910–1920. *Library of Congress, LC-D4–73453.*

children did when young determined their adult behavior. Unstructured street play, youth gangs, and commercial entertainment, reformers worried, corrupted urban youth. Children needed wholesome, structured play, supervised by trained recreation leaders. Was the playground movement a humanistic effort for city youth? Or was it a social control campaign promoting teamwork, obedience, and patriotism to train working-class youngsters for factory and office work? To what extent did working-class people shape the playground movement to meet their own needs?

One way to test these conflicting views is by doing a history of playgrounds and public recreation in a community. Begin with standard questions about decision making, budgets, and service equity. Did a city, school system, county, or a special purpose district provide recreation? How did the locality make this decision? Next, examine the facilities. Who designed and constructed them? What features and equipment did they have? Did the city provide small lots with sand boxes and swings or a large, sprawling park featuring field house, gymnasium, swimming pool, baseball fields, along with slides, swings, and other play equipment? Who made equipment choices?

What recreation programs did local government offer? How and why did they change over time? What explains officials' choices? Who designed and ran recreation activities? What were their backgrounds and goals? What was the predicted and actual clientele for public recreation programs? Preschool children? Elementary pupils? Teenagers? Midlife adults? Senior citizens? Did officials offer recreation for some age groups and not others? If so, why? How did residents respond to organized recreation? Did children, for example, accept or resist the structured play recreation professionals promoted? How many took part? Did controversies arise? What were they, and what was the outcome? In addition to general urban periodicals, like *American City, Survey, Charities and the Commons*, and *National Municipal Review*, one can draw on playground and recreation movement sources, such as the Playground Association of America's *Playground*. Interviews also can enrich historical accounts of local public recreation.

Parks and playgrounds were amenities, but waste collection and disposal were necessities. Although hardly glamorous, solid waste is an important part of local history. Waste includes garbage (organic waste), rubbish (other disposables), and furnace ash. As late as 1880, a majority of U.S. cities did not collect solid waste. By 1915, however, half did so directly and another two-fifths contracted with private scavengers. When did a local government make solid waste collection a public matter? Did it do so because growth increased its volume? Because of health concerns? For aesthetic reasons or for civic pride? Who led in making this decision? What role did professional experts play? Smaller communities lagged behind large ones and often required residents to bring waste to a central facility, often a county or township dumpsite.

Local government could either handle solid waste itself or hire private business to do it. In the 1980s, as landfill fees and public employee earnings jumped, many communities tried to cut costs by hiring private firms to pick up their trash. Large corporations like Browning-Ferris Industries and Waste Management bought out small local companies and sought government contracts. State and federal environmental regulations and grant procedures made solid waste issues more complex. Communities that did not yield garbage duties

Garbage trucks, Grand Rapids, Michigan, 1930s. *Perry W. Greene Papers, Bentley Historical Library, University of Michigan.*

to their county or to a special district often turned to private enterprise. Between 1987 and 1995, private firms' share of U.S. public waste collection rose from 30 percent to half. What did the public gain and lose by using private companies? What did any one community decide? What was the basis of this choice? Did its decision change over time?

After collection comes disposal. What methods did a locality use? Dumping in a river or ocean? On open land dumps? Feeding garbage to hogs? Burning it in incinerators? Converting it to oils, fertilizer, or energy? Establishing specially designed sanitary landfills? Putting refuse in reclamation projects, creating new land in low-lying areas and along lake and ocean shores? What benefits and problems occurred with each of these methods? For example, from the 1920s to the 1970s, officials placed six of Houston's eight incinerators and all five of its landfills in African American areas. After blacks got the right to vote in the 1960s, they used their ballots to resist such selective placement. Have residents contested waste disposal sites? Has the balance among cost, environmental impact, and public opinion changed over the years?

In recent decades, as disposable packaging increased solid waste volume, local governments tried to reverse the trend. What has a single community done? Has it imposed per-bag trash charges to encourage residents to throw out less? Launched publicly funded recycling programs? Started recycling in city offices? Bought recycled paper for government use? Promoted homeowner composting of yard and kitchen waste? Some places have required residents to separate grass clippings, weeds, and leaves from trash and have put yard waste in centralized compost sites. Recycling and source separation cost residents time and increased public collection budgets, but these measures also curbed trash collection and landfill costs. Cities and townships also earned some money from selling recycled newspaper, office paper, cardboard, paperboard, cans, glass, and plastic. Meanwhile, sink-mounted disposers and trash compactors have also cut garbage volume. How has the community balanced education and coercion for recycling and source separation? How have residents responded to changing demands about solid waste?

Another environmental issue to study is local government's response to air and noise pollution. Through the nineteenth century, city leaders welcomed smoke and noise, for they symbolized progress and prosperity. By the late nineteenth century, however, some felt city life had become unpleasant and dangerous. Smoke, particularly from bituminous coal, damaged lungs, buildings, clothing, and trees. Noise from factories, vehicles, and vendors was distracting or unhealthy. What made local people sensitive to these issues? Who led opposition to poor air and loud noise? What did government do? How effective was it? Did developments in other cities or at the national level shape what occurred in a particular community?

Those who choose local environmental history face several enduring issues. How did communities balance economic growth and environmental quality? Did the two conflict or were they compatible? Did government educate offenders and give them incentives to change? Or did it prosecute them? How well did each option work? Did technological change solve pollution problems? For example, air quality improved as natural gas and electricity heated homes and factories instead of coal. On the other hand, autos replaced horse wastes with harmful gases. Finally, which level of government enacted and enforced environmental regulations? Having multiple governments with overlapping authority made pollution control difficult.

Supplying water is another essential public service that merits local historians' efforts. Who provided water to the community? At first, people dug wells, collected rainwater, and took water from nearby rivers and lakes. As localities grew, private companies sold water to residents; some competed, but others were government-sponsored monopolies. Many U.S. water systems remain privately owned today, especially in small communities. The current popularity of bottled water shows the importance of private enterprise in supplying businesses and other affluent customers. Did a town create a public water system? How and why? Were epidemic diseases the catalyst? Scarcity from dry wells? How significant was soaring demand? Were factories, homes, or commercial establishments like hotels, laundries, and restaurants the biggest water users? Did major property owners and insurance companies push for a public water system? What were their motives? How important was improving the community's image in making the decision?

For each aspect of the history of public water, several common questions deserve attention. Who made the major decisions? How important were private businessmen? Elected officials? Appointed administrators? Technical experts? Did government employ its own engineers or did it hire private engineering firms temporarily or on long-term contracts? How has water technology changed? To what degree did technological demands shape decisions about the water system? How did a community administer its system? Did each city have its own water network? Did several of them form a special purpose district? Or did the county assume the task of supplying water?

Securing enough water was a major challenge for local government. Where did a community obtain its water? Has this changed over time? If so, how and why? One can document how much water

Water Works, Ypsilanti, Michigan, 1902. Most localities drew water from the nearest available source, be it a river, lake, or wells. Population and industrial growth, however, made water quantity and quality ongoing challenges. *Ypsilanti Historical Archives.*

Probing the History of Local Government Services 75

people used. How did the system fulfill ever-increasing demand? Here are a few examples. From the 1870s to the 1940s, Houston relied on wells. Its growth then required it to build a reservoir by damning the San Jacinto River. Some cities brought water from ever-greater distances. New York City pioneered here. From 1837–1842, it damned the Croton River and constructed a forty-mile aqueduct to Manhattan. By the 1890s, New York had to build a New Croton Aqueduct and the world's largest masonry dam. Two decades later, New Yorkers drew water 100 miles away from the Catskill Mountains. In the arid Southwest, officials went even farther. In the early 1900s, Los Angeles reached 200 miles for water from the Owens River Valley. Soon Los Angeles captured water from the Colorado River. Conflict over water supply was common in the twentieth-century West.

A second part of the story is how communities distributed water to users. When and how did a network of reservoirs, pumping stations, large mains, and smaller pipes develop? Did a town ever use street hydrants as end points for water distribution? When and why did it bring water into individual homes and businesses? Municipal distribution systems required planning, maintenance, and technical know-how. Did all areas of the town get city water at the same time? If not, when did officials provide service to each area? Explain differing patterns of water service in various parts of the community.

Discussing the fiscal history of local water is also useful. What were the major categories of expenses and revenues? How did government pay for operations and capital improvements? How did users pay for water? With flat fees? Based on how much they used? How did officials structure water rates? What rates, for example, did local government charge large industrial users? Tax-exempt institutions? Individual homeowners? It was costly to replace existing lines or serve new areas. Did the city issue bonds to fund expensive water improvements? If so, how did it finance principal and interest payments? If from property taxes, land owners paid proportionate to their assessments, but tax-exempt users did not pay for capital improvements, no matter how much water they used. Funding improvements on the basis of water use, on the other hand, angered powerful businesses, universities, and hospitals. What choices did a community make?

Water quality also attracts historians. How pure was water? What degraded water quality? When did a city filter or purify its water? Why did it do this? What method did it use and how effective was it? How did water treatment change over time? What was the local impact of federal legislation beginning with the Safe Water Drinking Act

Laying water main, Philadelphia, 1901. *City Archives of Philadelphia.*

Probing the History of Local Government Services 77

of 1974? Did new federal standards bring conflict or cooperation among neighboring cities, townships, and counties?

Water history can be technical, but it can also be emotional. What disagreements occurred in a specific locality about water? During the 1950s and 1960s, proposals to fluoridate water to retard tooth decay tore many communities apart. Medical expertise and health claims clashed with fears of outside control and communist subversion. Has water politics been prominent in the community? In what ways did water represent people's values, hopes, and anxieties? Water wars have reflected conflicts between economic growth and environmental quality, between local control and regional coordination, and between the individual and government.

Sewer and water systems are closely related and share similar histories. In most places, sewers were local government's largest construction projects. Like water, sewer networks include stories of technological change, engineering expertise, debt financing, deadly disease, environmental concerns, intergovernmental coordination, and enforcement of federal standards. The same questions about water history apply to a study of sewers. It makes sense to begin by describing conditions before sewers. People threw human and animal waste into streets, empty lots, and nearby waterways. They also built backyard cesspools and cellar privy vaults, which required frequent emptying by private scavengers. These methods ruined water quality, flooded backyards, and caused deadly epidemics. Cities became dirty and foul smelling.

Researchers can trace the origins of a local government's centralized sewer system, describing each of its components. Gutters in the middle or at sides of streets directed water to drains which fed small clay pipes and larger brick or concrete mains. These mains led to pumping stations powered by large steam engines. Some communities built separate systems for groundwater and wastewater, but most combined the two. This cost less but produced huge volumes of wastewater that cities dumped untreated into rivers and oceans. As a result, diseases like typhoid ended or ruined many lives.

Eventually, communities treated their sewage. Cities were slow to do this, since those who paid did not necessarily benefit directly. During the Great Depression, the U.S. government funded sewage treatment plants as job-creating public works projects. As a result, from 1930 to 1940, the proportion of U.S. city dwellers with sewage treatment soared from one-fourth to over half. In the 1960s and 1970s, federal water quality standards and federal money finally made wastewater treatment common. How does any one community fit in this picture? Did water and sewer systems influence annexation or other changes in municipal boundaries? Did the area operate a regional sewage treatment system? If so, what is its history?

Besides providing services, regulation is a major function of local government. As noted earlier, cities and townships enacted ordinances that restricted individuals and businesses to promote public order, health, and safety. Housing regulation is one example. Does your city, township, or county have a housing code? If not, why? If so, when was it enacted and why? Who favored its passage? What were their motives and arguments? Did advocates believe that bad housing was inhumane for inhabitants? Unhealthy or dangerous to all? Did they assert that better housing would improve people's behavior? Who opposed enactment of housing regulations? What did they say and why? Who gained from improved rental housing conditions? Who lost? How did landlords and tenants influence the adoption of housing codes? What does your code say? For example, Pennsylvania's 1903 law, which applied to Pittsburgh, limited residential structures to 80 percent of lot size, banned windowless rooms, specified minimum room size, and required indoor plumbing, ventilation, and hallway lighting. Which housing units did a code cover? Did it exclude any housing? If so, what and why? Besides public records and the press, records of local housing advocacy groups can shed light on this subject.

After discussing passage of rental housing regulation, it is wise to assess the results. One can do this by matching census and other survey data about housing conditions with building department and court records. Examine city or township budgets and departmental reports to see how much money and personnel officials devoted to housing inspection. Who enforced the code? How did they do it? Did local government have a regular inspection program? Describe its history and operation. Historians point out that some codes applied only to newly built housing, which left most buildings unregulated. Even where codes were comprehensive and enforcement strong, the supply of good quality affordable housing might not grow. In fact, by increasing the cost of cheap residences, codes might channel more private investment into high-cost housing. Did housing inspection accomplish what proponents and opponents predicted? How did landlords and tenants adjust to rental housing inspection? What impact did the codes have on the local rental market? How did the local political climate determine the program's outcome?

States, counties, and municipalities also adopted building codes covering construction standards. These laws regulated methods and

Probing the History of Local Government Services   79

materials for carpentry, roofing, plumbing, and electrical systems. To pursue this topic, one can adapt questions suggested in preceding paragraphs. What part did landlords, labor unions, builders, and real estate interests play in shaping construction codes? What was the relationship between building and rental housing codes? Who wrote the regulations a community adopted? Were the authors local, or did officials adopt codes written elsewhere?

Turning to enforcement, who were the city, township, or county housing and building inspectors? What were their backgrounds and training? Did local government treat all property owners and parts of the community similarly? What was the relationship between the building department and local government attorney regarding enforcement? Did building standards affect the amount, cost, and quality of housing locally? Some critics charge that building codes hurt technological change, protected large contractors and unions, and thus kept housing costs high. Does evidence support this? A historian should examine building permits and inspection records, as well as evidence from private interest groups.

Some cities went beyond regulation and entered the housing market directly. In 1937, the Wagner-Steagall Act created the United States Housing Authority, which pledged federal grants and loans to cities that started agencies to house the poor. Federal funds paid up to nine-tenths of the cost of buying and clearing land and building the housing; Washington also subsidized ongoing operations. Cities completed some units in the late 1930s and many more in the 1950s and 1960s. By then, the federal government added new public housing programs. It earmarked money for low-income senior citizen housing and authorized vouchers paying for poor people to rent privately owned units.

Does a city have public housing? If not, was it proposed and rejected? Who supported and who opposed public housing; what arguments did each side make? How did local elected officials respond? Did the issue generate public interest? Did low-income people join the debate? Who appointed the public housing commission? What were members' backgrounds, ideas, and economic interests? Who served as appointed public housing administrators? What were their policies, achievements, and failings?

Though Washington helped pay for public housing, it left many decisions in local hands. Site selection was crucial. Who decided the location of public housing in a city? What was the process? Where did officials put public housing? Why did they choose those sites? Did authorities build low-income housing on vacant land? Or did they

Children at Stateway Gardens Public Housing Project, Chicago, 1973. Highly contested questions of race, class, and the role of government have infused the history of public housing from its origins in the 1930s to the present. *National Archives, Record Group 412, Environmental Protection Agency, NWDNS-412-DA-13711.*

demolish existing buildings? If so, what did they tear down? Federal guidelines promised relocation aid for those who lost their homes to slum clearance. Did this occur in the locality under consideration?

Tenant selection also merits investigation. What guidelines regarding age, income, employment, and family structure did officials use? Were such criteria national or local? Were tenants employed or jobless? Two-parent families or single female heads of households? What was the proportion of children? The elderly? Did these change over time? If so, how and why? What racial patterns appeared? What percentage of public housing residents were African American? Hispanic? Asian? Native American? What customs and policies on race did the housing agency follow? Was public housing racially segregated or integrated? Did public housing shape racial patterns in the city?

Finally, researchers can consider public housing architecture and its social effects. Did a city build clusters of two- or three-story buildings with multiple entrances? High-rise structures with elevators? What were the results of each design? How did tenants relate to each other and to management? Did they organize, either independently or under management sponsorship? What social or institutional networks developed among residents?

Besides housing, many local governments provide public transportation. In mass transit, large numbers of riders travel on fixed routes and schedules for a standard fare. Mass transit began in New York City in the late 1820s with competing drivers of horse-drawn wagons called omnibuses. By the end of the nineteenth century, large corporations ran electric-powered trolleys, cable cars, subways, and elevated railways in North American cities. At this time, cities had legal and regulatory relations with mass transit. Cities granted exclusive franchises to private companies, regulated fares and service, and received annual fees. A century ago, mass transit was a major local issue, with companies, elected officials, and consumers arguing over fares, service, and payoffs for franchise awards. Cleveland's Mayor Tom Johnson (1901–1909), a former transit owner, called streetcar firms a major source of corruption and urged cities to take them over.

Cities eventually took Johnson's advice, although under different circumstances. More and more people deserted trolleys or buses, preferring the speed, privacy, comfort, and flexibility of autos. From the 1920s, mass transit ridership fell, so fares rose and service deteriorated. As private transit firms weakened, cities bought them and made them public. By the 1970s, nine-tenths of U.S. transit passengers used public systems. In the case of mass transit, capitalism was

Riders waiting for streetcar, Oklahoma City, 1939. Library of Congress, LC-USF33–012342-M4-DLC.

for successful businesses, socialism for failed ones. Is public mass transit part of a city's history? If so, the researcher might measure this overview against local experience.

ༀ ༀ ༀ ༀ ༀ

THE POLITICS OF PUBLIC TRANSPORTATION: ATLANTA IN THE 1960s AND 1970s

Urban commuters hope their bus or train arrives on time and they can get a seat. Local historians, though, use public transportation to learn about their community. Georgia Institute of Technology historian Ronald Bayor and University of Maryland political scientist Clarence Stone show this in separate accounts of the politics of mass transit in Atlanta.

When President Lyndon Johnson's Great Society offered federal

Probing the History of Local Government Services

Passengers and MARTA train, Atlanta, 1996. *Photo by author.*

funds for mass transit in the 1960s, Atlanta businessmen convinced Georgia to establish MARTA (Metropolitan Atlanta Rapid Transit Authority). Downtown leaders hoped a modern rail network would bring affluent North Siders to the central business district, boosting its retail sales, tax base, and property values.

Since MARTA financing required voter approval, corporate leaders needed political allies. Black Atlanta was a likely partner. By the late 1960s, African Americans were half Atlanta's population and two-fifths of its voters. They often gave political support to local big business. Blacks relied on mass transit more than whites but had major grievances about it. Until a 1959 federal court ruling, they had to sit in separate sections on local buses. Furthermore, their neighborhoods had poor bus service, so shopping and getting to work were inconvenient. When at first pro-MARTA forces ignored their concerns, blacks helped defeat MARTA's rapid transit proposal in a 1968 referendum.

After that, MARTA promised African American leaders that 35 percent of transit jobs and contracts would go to black workers and minority-owned businesses. MARTA also agreed to improve bus service, build an east-west rail route to serve black residents, and construct a Proctor Creek Spur to serve Perry Homes, a black housing project on Atlanta's northwest side. Blacks were less successful on fiscal policy. They preferred funding transit through an income tax, which would fall lightly on low-income people. Instead, MARTA, courting suburban voters, chose a financially regressive 1 percent sales tax. To appeal to African Americans, however, MARTA promised ultra-low 15-cent bus fares for seven years.

Meanwhile, predominantly white, auto-oriented suburbanites balked at paying for a rail system they felt mainly served city residents. In addition, suburbanites feared high-speed rapid transit would bring blacks into their suburbs to work, attend school, and live. As a result, suburban Gwinnett and Clayton Counties did not join MARTA.

Despite this setback, the business-black coalition won a majority for MARTA in Fulton (Atlanta) and DeKalb Counties in a second 1971 referendum. Business leaders got their downtown-centered rapid transit network. Though MARTA did not keep all its pledges to blacks, they nonetheless won most demands for better service and more jobs and minority business contracts. Stone's and Bayor's research used mass transit as a window on one city's struggle with difficult issues of race, class, downtown retailing, and urban-suburban relations.

In his work, Stone relied primarily on University of Georgia political scientists' reports to the U.S. Department of Transportation and on a thesis by a Princeton University undergraduate. Bayor based his account on MARTA's papers at the Atlanta Historical Society and on coverage in the *Atlanta Journal* and *Atlanta Constitution*, the city's major white-owned papers, and the *Atlanta Daily World*, operated and read by African Americans.

Sources: Ronald H. Bayor, *Race and the Shaping of Twentieth-Century Atlanta* (Chapel Hill: University of North Carolina Press, 1996), and Clarence N. Stone, *Regime Politics: Governing Atlanta, 1946–1988* (Lawrence: University Press of Kansas, 1989).

༄༅ ༄༅ ༄༅ ༄༅ ༄༅

In providing amenities like parks, recreation, and transit, local government provided direct benefits to residents. That is one definition of the welfare state, a concept at the center of spirited policy debates. These arguments concern human nature, the value of work, the role of the state, social class, and race—all of which evoke strong feelings. Historians can join this debate by learning how local government reacted to poverty or what benefits a city or county gave the poor, the affluent, or businesses. Surprising conclusions may emerge. For one thing, poor people were not the only nor even the largest beneficiaries

Probing the History of Local Government Services 85

of the welfare state. Second, the story starts in colonial times, not in the 1930s New Deal or the 1960s Great Society. Third, many poor people got little or no government aid. Finally, if welfare or the welfare state means government providing benefits or services for which others pay, this describes much of what we ask of government. When we stroll in the park, flush our toilets, or drive down the street, our benefit from government exceeds our cost.

Many are unaware of how generous government is to the nonpoor. Nationally, tax credits and deductions, corporate subsidies, mortgage guarantees, and social entitlements have given big benefits to middle-class and upper-class people. Local governments used the property tax system to help business. Cities and townships gave businesses tax abatements on equipment (classified as personal property) and real estate to induce them to come or to stay. This saved recipients big sums of money and shifted local government costs to those without abatements. Local officials also often deliberately underassessed business property. Did a locality grant tax abatements? If so, how many and why? What did businesses do to get one? What were the results for business and for the community? How did the tax assessor treat major apartment, retail, and industrial property owners?

Local government also practiced corporate welfare by helping finance privately owned ventures. Did the city or county give or loan money to railroads or canal companies? To manufacturers? Did it build roads, sewers, or other infrastructure for which other taxpayers paid? Did local government give special services to business without charge? Did it, for example, help big industries by subduing strikes? Did it assist concert promoters or professional sports teams with traffic and crowd control? Did the public support such aid or did it stir controversy?

When most people think about welfare, they mean public aid to the needy. English law assigned poor relief to local government. American colonists limited aid to long-time residents, auctioned poor people to employers, and paid families to take dependent people into their homes. By the 1660s, larger towns and cities opened almshouses. Their residents sometimes worked, which gave them something to do and helped offset costs. Most public aid recipients, though, got "outdoor relief" of food, clothes, and firewood. Poor relief was a big share of municipal spending in eighteenth-century America.

What did a community's public officials in the past believe about the causes of poverty? Did they attribute it to economic forces like industrialization and deindustrialization? Or was the character or behavior of the poor themselves responsible? If so, could the poor change? What would change them? One might identify changes and continuity in attitudes about poverty and the poor.

Did a local government assist the poor? If so, in what ways? Colonial-era strategies persist today: encouraging the needy to go away, housing them in institutions, putting them to work, and giving them cash or in-kind charity. Did the community have a poorhouse (often called a county farm)? Did it maintain other institutions for dependents, such as orphans, the blind, and the mentally ill? Who lived here? Who ran them? What occurred there? What sort of "outdoor" or noninstitutional aid did the city or county offer the needy? Did it house homeless at police stations? Did it operate municipal lodging houses? Offer in-kind or cash charity? Did your city create public service jobs for the poor? During the 1890s depression, for instance, Detroit Mayor Hazen Pingree hired the jobless to pave and sweep streets, expand water and sewer lines, and improve the park on Belle Isle; he also encouraged them to grow food on vacant lots. Did a community's relief programs change over time? If so, how and why? Did the city take special measures to help people in times of economic collapse? With what results?

For the twentieth century, several themes warrant attention. First, cities and counties created local welfare bureaucracies. Investigators can trace the history of a county or municipal welfare department. What information and conclusions emerge about its leadership, administration, budget, services, and strategy toward the needy?

A second trail leads to interplay between public and private charity. For example, some nineteenth-century cities had privately run dispensaries, health clinics for the poor, which accepted both public and individual contributions. Orphanages operated the same way. By the twentieth century, public hospitals replaced dispensaries and federal Aid to Families with Dependent Children (1935) reduced orphanage occupancy. Today cities still contract with private agencies to provide everything from health services for teenagers to respite care for the frail elderly, from drug abuse treatment to emergency intervention hotlines. How have the public and private sectors in a community allocated their welfare activities? What religious, ethnic, or racial sponsorship and standards did these agencies have? How did local government accommodate such affiliations? Did the government buy specific services from these agencies or donate unearmarked funds? Did these private organizations issue financial or activity reports to the public?

The rise and decline of federal government welfare for the poor is a third development. The story begins with Roosevelt's New Deal in the

1930s, when Washington launched both temporary relief and ongoing welfare programs. Did the Federal Emergency Relief Administration operate in a particular community? Did the area have WPA (Works Progress Administration), CCC (Civilian Conservation Corps), or NYA (National Youth Administration) work relief projects? Trace relations between local and federal government. Who decided how federal money was spent? Who set eligibility requirements and decided what the needy would get? Who supervised work crews? How did federally funded projects change a community?

Those interested in the less distant past can adapt these questions to the War on Poverty during Lyndon Johnson's administration (1963–1969). Study a local government's involvement in low-income housing, job training, urban revitalization, or community action. One can also interpret the growth of a local welfare bureaucracy in the 1960s and 1970s. What new state programs in public health, mental health, and education appeared in your county or city? For either state or federal programs, did implementation differ from design? What unforeseen problems arose? Did interests that lost out in Washington or at the state capital assert themselves locally? Moving closer to the present, was the war on welfare of the 1980s and 1990s fought at the local level? Who fought it and with what arguments and weapons? Have state and national welfare policy changes affected local government? Has resistance to change occurred? If so, from where did it come?

Although this chapter has served an extensive menu of topics to consider, it has offered a mere sample of local government services, not a complete listing. Cities, townships, and counties have carried out a wide range of activities, from inspecting food to lending books, from delivering babies to killing rats and gypsy moths. The daily experience of life in any community can generate additional research possibilities, especially those distinct to a single area.

In doing research, it would be wise to exploit as many as possible of the sources mentioned in Chapter 2. In addition to that general listing of secondary sources, public records, newspapers and magazines, state and federal censuses, interviews, artifacts and structures, be sure to draw on sources specific to each topic. Professional associations, labor unions, businesses, and trade groups keep archives and publish newsletters. For instance, scientific, engineering, and medical periodicals covered everything from street construction to public health to air pollution. Landscape design magazines illuminated park development, while social work journals publicized playgrounds and covered welfare. For example, Martin Melosi, an urban environmental historian, used general interest newspapers and periodicals like *New York Times, Outlook,* and *Harper's Weekly;* technical books on waste disposal; and specialized journals like *Scientific American, American Journal of Public Health,* and *Municipal Journal and Engineer.* To locate professional and technical sources, talk to a reference librarian, particularly at a university or large public library.

As this chapter has shown, local government touches much of daily life. A city, township, or county's services have rich histories. Each sheds light on what makes a community stand out but also identifies common trends in the development of North American communities. Individuals make public decisions and deliver services through government. Politics, on the other hand, is the process of selecting decision makers and making choices. The next section suggests ways to learn more about doing the history of that process.

SUGGESTED READINGS

Christine Meisner Rosen offers a framework for analyzing urban services in "Infrastructural Improvement in Nineteenth-Century Cities: A Conceptual Framework and Cases," *Journal of Urban History,* 12 (May, 1986), 211–256; see also her book, *The Limits of Power: Great Fires and the Process of City Growth in America* (Cambridge: Cambridge University Press, 1986). Olivier Zunz, *The Changing Face of Inequality: Urbanization, Industrial Development, and Immigrants in Detroit, 1880–1920* (Chicago: University of Chicago Press, 1982), and Roger D. Simon, "Housing and Services in an Immigrant Neighborhood: Milwaukee's Ward 14," *Journal of Urban History,* 2 (August, 1976), 435–458, document unequal distribution of city services. Michael W. Homel, *Down From Equality: Black Chicagoans and the Public Schools, 1920–1941* (Urbana: University of Illinois Press, 1984), traces the rise of educational inequality in a major northern city.

For police history, see two articles by Eric Monkkonen, "From Cop History to Social History: The Significance of the Police in American History," *Journal of Social History,* 15 (Summer, 1982), 575–587, and "History of Urban Police," in Michael Tonry and Norval Morris, eds., *Modern Policing* (Chicago: University of Chicago Press, 1992), 547–580, and one by James F. Richardson, "Police History: The Search for Legitimacy," *Journal of Urban History,* 6 (February, 1980), 231–246. Two more introductions are David R. Johnson, *American Law Enforcement: A History* (St. Louis: Forum Press, 1981), and Richardson's *Urban Police in the United States* (Port Washington, NY: Kennikat Press, 1974). For individual cities, see Johnson's *Policing the Urban Underworld: The Impact of Crime on the Development of the American Police, 1800–1887* (Philadelphia: Temple University Press, 1979), Richardson's *The New York Police: Colonial Times to 1801* (New York: Oxford University Press, 1970), and Roger Lane, *Policing the City: Boston, 1822–1885* (Cambridge, MA: Harvard University Press, 1967). For police in the twentieth century, see Robert M. Fogelson, *Big-City Police* (Cambridge, MA: Harvard University Press, 1977), Jonathan Rubenstein, *City Police* (New York: Farrar, Straus, and Giroux, 1974), and James Q. Wilson, *Varieties of Police Behavior* (Cambridge, MA: Harvard University Press, 1968).

While fine scholarly work on police abounds, academic work on fire fighting is slimmer. See Amy Greenberg, *Cause for Alarm: The Volunteer Fire Department in the Nineteenth-Century City* (Princeton, NJ: Princeton University Press, 1998), and Teaford, *The Unheralded Triumph,* cited earlier.

For streets, see Clay McShane, "Transforming the Use of Urban Space: A Look at the Revolution in Street Pavements, 1880–1924," *Journal of Urban History,* 5 (May, 1979), 279–307; "Urban Pathways: The Street and the Highway, 1900–1940," in Joel A. Tarr and Gabriel Dupuy, eds., *Technology and the Rise of the Networked City in Europe and America* (Philadelphia: Temple University Press, 1988), pp. 67–87; and McShane's book, *Down the Asphalt Path: The Automobile and the American City* (New York: Columbia University Press, 1994). Two other works on the automobile's conquest of urban streets are Paul Barrett, *The Automobile and Urban Transit: The Formation of Public Policy in Chicago, 1900–1930* (Philadelphia: Temple University Press, 1983), and Mark S. Foster, *From Streetcar to Superhighway: American City Planners and Urban Transportation, 1900–1940* (Philadelphia: Temple University Press, 1981). The story of St. Louis's gated communities appears in David Beito, "Owning the 'Commanding Heights': Historical Perspectives on Private Streets," in "Public-Private Partnerships: Privatization in Historical Perspective," *Essays in Public Works History,* 16 (1990).

The literature on urban expressways attempts to keep pace with the number of automobiles on them. Leading studies include Bruce E. Seely, *Building the American Highway System: Engineers as Policy Makers* (Philadelphia: Temple University Press, 1987), and Mark H. Rose, *Interstate: Express Highway Politics, 1939–1989* (Knoxville: University of Tennessee Press, rev. ed., 1990). See also Cliff Ellis, "Professional Conflict over Urban Form: The Case of Urban Freeways, 1930 to 1970," in Mary Corbin Sies and Christopher Silver, eds., *Planning the*

Twentieth-Century American City (Baltimore: Johns Hopkins University Press, 1996), and Raymond A. Mohl, "Race and Space in the Modern City: Interstate-95 and the Black Community in Miami," in Arnold R. Hirsch and Raymond A. Mohl, eds., *Urban Policy in Twentieth-Century America* (New Brunswick, NJ: Rutgers University Press, 1993). For a case study of how a bridge shaped urban growth, see Eugene P. Moehring, "Space, Economic Growth, and the Public Works Revolution in New York," in *Infrastructure and Urban Growth in the Nineteenth Century* (Chicago: Public Works Historical Society, 1985).

For New York City's Central Park, see Moehring's article cited above. A prize-winning history is Roy Rosenzweig and Elizabeth Blackmar, *The Park and the People: A History of Central Park* (Ithaca, NY: Cornell University Press, 1992). Rosenzweig's *Eight Hours For What We Will: Workers and Leisure in an Industrial City, 1870-1920* (Cambridge: Cambridge University Press, 1983), explores immigrant culture and mass culture; urban parks are part of his account. David Schuyler provides a fine overview of the creation of urban parks in *The New Urban Landscape: The Redefinition of City Form in Nineteenth-Century America* (Baltimore: Johns Hopkins University Press, 1986). William L. Wilson's valuable work on city planning history, *The City Beautiful Movement* (Baltimore: Johns Hopkins University Press, 1989), continues where Schuyler leaves off; Wilson's coverage of urban parks emphasizes Seattle and Kansas City. See also Galen Cranz, *The Politics of Park Design: A History of Urban Parks in America* (Cambridge: Massachusetts Institute of Technology Press, 1982), and Glen E. Holt, "Private Plans for Public Spaces: The Origins of Chicago's Park System, 1850-1875," *Chicago History*, 8 (Fall, 1979), 173-184.

Urban recreation and playground movements have their historians as well. Begin with Dominick Cavallo, *Muscles and Morals: Organized Playgrounds and Urban Reform, 1880-1920* (Philadelphia: University of Pennsylvania Press, 1981), and Paul Boyer, *Urban Masses and Moral Order in America, 1820-1920* (Cambridge, MA: Harvard University Press, 1978). Stephen Hardy and Alan G. Ingham provide an overview of the issues in "Games, Structures, and Agency: Historians on the American Play Movement," *Journal of Social History*, 17 (Winter, 1983), 285-301. For a case study, see Joan E. Draper, "The Art and Science of Park Planning in the United States: Chicago's Small Parks, 1902 to 1905," in Mary Corbin Sies and Christopher Silver, eds., *Planning the Twentieth-Century American City* (Baltimore: Johns Hopkins University Press, 1996).

To enter the vast topic of urban infrastructure, begin with the first volume in the Exploring Community History Series, Ann Durkin

Keating's *Invisible Networks: Exploring the History of Local Utilities and Public Works* (Malabar, FL: Krieger, 1994). A comprehensive critical review of work in the field is Eugene P. Moehring, *Public Works and Urban History: Recent Trends and New Directions* (Chicago: Public Works Historical Society, 1982). Suellen M. Hoy, Michael C. Robinson, and Ellis L. Armstrong, eds., *History of Public Works in the United States, 1776–1976* (Chicago: American Public Works Association, 1976), and Hoy and Robinson, *Public Works History in the United States: A Guide to the Literature* (Nashville, TN: American Association for State and Local History, 1982) are rich sources. Tarr and Dupuy, eds., *Technology and the Rise of the Networked City in Europe and America*, cited above, is an edited collection of articles with a comparative perspective.

The leading historian of urban pollution is Martin V. Melosi. For solid waste, see his *Garbage in the Cities: Refuse, Reform, and the Environment, 1880–1980* (College Station: Texas A&M University Press, 1981). Melosi also edited a collection of articles entitled *Pollution and Reform in American Cities, 1870–1930* (Austin: University of Texas Press, 1980). Suellen Hoy, *Chasing Dirt: The American Pursuit of Cleanliness* (New York: Oxford University Press, 1995), contains a section on the Progressive Era drive for clean cities. For a case study about solid waste, sewer, and water, see Melosi's article, "Sanitary Services and Decision Making in Houston, 1876–1945," in *Journal of Urban History*, 20 (May, 1994), 365–406.

Two historical treatments of air and noise pollution are R. Dale Grinder, "The Battle for Clean Air: The Smoke Problem in Post–Civil War America," and Raymond W. Smilor, "Toward an Environmental Perspective: The Anti-Noise Campaign, 1893–1932," both in Melosi, ed., *Pollution and Reform in American Cities, 1870–1930* (Austin: University of Texas Press, 1980).

The classic history of urban water is Nelson Manfred Blake, *Water for the Cities: A History of the Urban Water Supply Problem in the United States* (Syracuse, NY: Syracuse University Press, 1958). For briefer, more modern accounts, consult Stuart Galishoff, "Triumph and Failure: The American Response to the Urban Water Supply Problem, 1860–1923," in Melosi, ed., *Pollution and Reform in American Cities*; Letty Anderson, "Fire and Disease: The Development of Water Supply Systems in New England, 1870–1900," in Tarr and Dupuy, eds., *Technology and the Rise of the Networked City in Europe and America*; and Moehring, *Public Works and Urban History*, all cited above. Margaret Leslie Davis, *Rivers in the Desert: William Mulholland and the Inventing of Los Angeles* (New York: HarperCollins, 1993), tells the story of the Owens River Valley project.

For sewers, in addition to the Moehring, Melosi, and Keating works cited above, see Joel A. Tarr, James McCurley, and Terry F. Yosie, "The Development and Impact of Urban Wastewater Technology: Changing Concepts of Water Quality Control, 1850–1930," in Melosi, ed., *Pollution and Reform in American Cities;* Tarr, "Sewerage and the Development of the Networked City in the United States, 1850–1930," in Tarr and Dupuy, eds., *Technology and the Rise of the Networked City in Europe and America;* and Tarr, "The Separate vs. Combined Sewer Problem: A Case Study in Urban Technology Design Choice," *Journal of Urban History,* 5 (May, 1979), 308–339.

For housing, begin with these general histories: Gwendolyn Wright, *Building the Dream: A Social History of Housing in America* (New York: Pantheon, 1981), and Clifford Edward Clark, Jr., *The American Family Home: 1800–1960* (Chapel Hill: University of North Carolina Press, 1986). Robert G. Barrows, "Beyond the Tenement: Patterns of American Urban Housing, 1870–1930," *Journal of Urban History,* 9 (August, 1983), 395–420, provides a statistical survey of cities. For local government and housing, consult two books by Roy Lubove, *Twentieth-Century Pittsburgh: Government, Business, and Environmental Change* (New York: Wiley, 1969), and *The Progressives and the Slums: Tenement House Reform in New York City, 1890–1917* (Pittsburgh: University of Pittsburgh Press, 1962). Ronald Lawson, ed., *The Tenant Movement in New York City, 1904–1984* (New Brunswick, NJ: Rutgers University Press, 1986), treats renter activism, politics, and public policy in the U.S.'s largest city.

A brief introduction to public housing appears in Kenneth T. Jackson, *Crabgrass Frontier: The Suburbanization of the United States* (New York: Oxford University Press, 1985). For more detailed studies, see Devereux Bowley, Jr., *The Poorhouse: Subsidized Housing in Chicago, 1895–1976* (Carbondale: Southern Illinois University Press, 1978), and John F. Bauman, *Public Housing, Race, and Renewal: Urban Planning in Philadelphia, 1920–1974* (Philadelphia: Temple University Press, 1987). See also John F. Bauman, Norman P. Hummon, and Edward K. Muller, "Public Housing, Isolation, and the Urban Underclass: Philadelphia's Richard Allen Homes, 1941–1965," *Journal of Urban History,* 17 (May, 1991), 264–292. For Miami, see the Mohl article cited above and his "Trouble in Paradise: Race and Housing in Miami during the New Deal Era," *Prologue: The Journal of the National Archives,* 19 (Spring, 1987), 7–21.

An early account of urban mass transit is John Anderson Miller, *Fares, Please! A Popular History of Trolleys, Horse-Cars, Street-Cars, Buses, Elevateds, and Subways* (orig. ed., 1941; second ed., New York: Dover,

1960). For the private-ownership era, two scholarly books are Charles Cheape, *Moving the Masses: Urban Public Transit in New York, Boston, and Philadelphia, 1880–1912* (Cambridge, MA: Harvard University Press, 1980), and Clay McShane, *Technology and Reform: Street Railways and the Growth of Milwaukee, 1887–1900* (Madison: State Historical Society of Wisconsin, 1974).

The literature on poverty and welfare is enormous. Begin with Walter I. Trattner, *From Poor Law to Welfare State: A History of Social Welfare in America* (2nd ed., New York: Free Press, 1979); Michael B. Katz, *In the Shadow of the Poorhouse: A Social History of Welfare In America* (New York: Basic Books, 1986); and James T. Patterson, *America's Struggle Against Poverty, 1900–1980* (Cambridge, MA: Harvard University Press, 1981). Frances Fox Piven and Richard A. Cloward, *Regulating the Poor: The Functions of Public Welfare* (New York: Pantheon, 1971), is provocative. Katz has also edited *The "Underclass" Debate: Views from History* (Princeton, NJ: Princeton University Press, 1993), a collection of essays, some about local government. Raymond A. Mohl's "Poverty in the Cities: A History of Urban Social Welfare," in Mohl and Richardson, eds., *The Urban Experience: Themes in American History* (Belmont, CA: Wadsworth, 1973), is a convenient overview with an urban emphasis. Marilyn T. Williams, *Washing "The Great Unwashed": Public Baths in Urban America, 1840–1920* (Columbus: Ohio State University Press, 1991), tells a largely forgotten story.

PART III
EXPLORING LOCAL POLITICS

Chapter 5

UNCOVERING THE HISTORY OF URBAN POLITICS

The structure and activities of local government are the products of decisions each community has made in the past. Politics is the process of making these public decisions. Through politics, voters decide who controls government, what it does, and how to pay for it. Defined more broadly, politics refers to how people decide things anywhere—in families and churches, at work, and in community groups.

Americans' skepticism about politics and politicians is deeply rooted. In part, public mistrust stems from dishonest or unethical things some candidates and elected officials do. Also, people yearn for harmony and consensus, but politics includes open disagreement. People disparage elected officials for failing to solve problems, even as they limit government's ability to do so. Finally, since politics is public and under media scrutiny, people learn more about politicians' faults. Because politics is so important, individuals should go beyond simply condemning it. The better people understand politics, the more likely they are to make it serve their needs.

Academic scholars have offered models for understanding local politics. Examining post–World War II Atlanta, political scientist Floyd Hunter found that a "power structure" made up of a few business leaders ran the city. After observing New Haven, Connecticut, Robert Dahl, another political scientist, argued that competing interest groups shared decision making. Historians have applied these two models to the past. In his book on Birmingham, Alabama, from the 1870s to the 1920s, Carl V. Harris combined Hunter and Dahl. Harris concluded that though a small clique of rich men held most elected positions, public decisions usually reflected conflicting needs of Birmingham's different population groups. David Hammack's portrait of New York City at the turn of the twentieth century leaned toward Dahl. Hammack pointed to the disunity of powerful elites, the rising influence of immigrants and workers, and the expanding role of technical experts.

Historians can test Hunter's and Dahl's concepts or formulate new ones by considering political power in any community. An opinion survey and conversation with a broad sample of residents can answer who the public thinks has power today or had it in the recent past. But who actually held political power? Local biographies, city directories, and census lists document elected officials' occupations and property holdings. Another approach is to trace the history of some policy decisions to find out who shaped the outcome. It would seem best to cite a number of different cases to get the most accurate answer. A history of the "web of influence" in a town may spark lively discussion.

As they explored questions of power, urban historians identified different styles or models of local politics. The actual situation rarely fit any of these models exactly, and features from different models often overlapped. Moreover, not every pattern appeared in each city, nor did patterns follow in predictable sequence. New suburbs, small towns, and big cities had different political histories, and the politics of cities in each category varied. Nevertheless, researchers can apply the discussion in this chapter to a local experience.

As Floyd Hunter found long ago in Atlanta, rule by the economically powerful is one type of local politics. Large retail and wholesale merchants, manufacturers, bankers, and real estate interests dominated politics and government in many, perhaps most, communities. Why was this? Business elites had the money, time, and organizational skills for public affairs. Some business people felt a duty or obligation to contribute to civic life. Also, many realized business success depended on local prosperity. Finally, those with wealth and property knew government could help or harm them. How did a city or township affect business? What demands for services did business people make on government? When did they want government to assert regulatory and police powers? When did they oppose use of these powers? What taxation policies did businesses want? How much political influence did a community's business leaders have? How did they wield their influence? Researchers can document answers both for government (legislative and administrative decisions) and for politics (choosing candidates and funding campaigns).

Business power in politics and government is a complex matter. As David Hammack found in New York City of 1900, business was not always unified. Very likely historians can identify and explain conflicting interests and views among a community's business leaders. Second, business people also act on their noneconomic identities. Further-

Uncovering the History of Urban Politics 99

more, as national and global corporations became dominant, bankers, merchants, and manufacturers in Tumwater, Washington, or Dothan, Alabama, weighed local values against national trends and directives from corporate headquarters. In fact, many "local" business leaders in the late twentieth century had shallow roots in their communities.

Another local political style is the "machine." "Boss" and "machine," of course, are pejoratives; participants referred to "the organization" or "the party" and used party titles, like precinct captain and ward committeeman. At their peak from about 1870 to 1940, neighborhood-based, highly organized parties or factions traded jobs, services, and favors for votes and money. Issues were normally secondary to winning power and enjoying its rewards. Contrary to their labels, most political organizations were not centralized dictatorships. Rather, they were coalitions or federations of local party groupings that tried, not always successfully, to put consensus above individual ambition. They often had business support, and some won the allegiance of middle-income residents. Nevertheless, political organizations were usually

Big-city political party members campaigning for a local judicial candidate, Chicago, n.d. *Chicago Historical Society, Henry Delorval Green Papers, Box 13.*

strongest among working-class and immigrant voters in older parts of cities. And their leaders, usually men of modest origins, were small businessmen or professionals based in ethnic communities.

What made "bosses" and "machines" possible? Poor newcomers needed a helping hand. Explosive economic development and population growth required more infrastructure and public services. As sons of earlier business leaders moved to suburbs or devoted all their time to making money, full-time politicians filled the gap. With local government weak and fragmented, professional politicians got things done—welcoming new arrivals, aiding the needy, and building streets, bridges, water mains, and public buildings.

KANSAS CITY'S PENDERGAST MACHINE: FROM THE WEST BOTTOMS TO THE WHITE HOUSE

Urban political organizations flourished not only in older northeastern cities but also in the South, the Midwest, and on the West Coast. Relying mainly on local newspapers and manuscript collections, historian Lyle Dorsett described the rise and fall of the Pendergast machine in Kansas City, Missouri, from the 1890s to the 1930s.

In 1876, Jim Pendergast came to Kansas City as a young unskilled laborer, joining other native whites, blacks, and Irish and German immigrants crowding the industrial West Bottoms. With winnings from a horseracing bet, Pendergast bought a saloon-hotel in the Bottoms and jumped into Democratic politics. He pleased working-class neighbors by cashing paychecks, finding them jobs, and giving the needy food and coal. Pendergast also protected gambling, which people enjoyed and from which he profited. Elected to the city council in 1892, Jim still did personal favors, but now he also used government to defend the working class. He forced utility firms to reduce rates, blocked a cut in firefighters' pay, and helped expand public services, like parks, boulevards, and the water system.

By the early 1900s, Jim Pendergast spread his influence from the West Bottoms into the nearby North End. As his health declined, he trained his younger brother Tom to take his place. After Jim died in 1911, Tom increased the machine's reach, allying with or subduing other politicians. By the 1920s, he grew rich from businesses that got public contracts and from prostitution and liquor payoffs. Meanwhile, Tom won outlying neighborhoods by backing a reform charter, by organizing middle-class Democratic clubs that held sporting and social events, and by sponsoring wholesome candidates, like Jackson

County Judge Harry Truman. In the late 1930s, election fraud and tax evasion broke Tom's organization and ended his career. By that time, however, his protege Truman held a U.S. Senate seat. In 1944, President Franklin Roosevelt chose Truman as his running mate. When FDR died in April, 1945, the son of the Pendergast machine claimed the White House's Oval Office. A path from the lowly West Bottoms led to the world's most powerful position.

Source: Lyle W. Dorsett, *The Pendergast Machine* (New York: Oxford University Press, 1968).

༃༅ ༃༅ ༃༅ ༃༅ ༃༅

Did a nearby city have a style of politics similar to Dorsett's Kansas City? If so, why did this occur? Who were the leaders? What were their backgrounds and goals? How successful were they? What explains their successes and failures? Describe their political organization. How did they win elections? Once gaining power, how did they keep it? Besides tangible aid like the Pendergasts gave, how else did politicians win voter loyalty? What policies did they favor or oppose? Did they attend wakes, funerals, weddings, church carnivals, and ethnic celebrations? Did they hold picnics, day trips, and sporting events? How did they finance their political organization? From payments by public employees? Contributions by legal businesses, large and small? Payoffs from illegal businesses? What did donors get for their money?

It is useful to assess the scope of a local political organization. Notice whether it flourished in one part of a city or county or if it covered much or most of the locality. Explain the findings. Why, for example, did the organization remain limited to a small area? Or how did it expand and appeal to several parts of the community? What problems arose as the organization tried to broaden its influence? Did drawing support from competing classes, races, or ethnic groups cause difficulties for the organization? If so, how did it deal with these tensions? Who remained outside the organization and why? Did pro- and antimachine opinion reflect social class, race, religion, or ethnicity? Moral or cultural views? Place of residence?

Researchers can also evaluate a local political organization's impact. How did it change the community? Perhaps it brought new people into government, enacted certain policies, or built public buildings, parks, and other infrastructure. Was the cost worth the achievement? Did the political organization persist? If so, how did it change? If it declined or collapsed, why? Corruption brought Pendergast down. Did a local community experience this as well? Dishonesty alone does not explain why organization politics weakened during the last half-century. Central city (and especially inner-city) populations fell. White ethnics gradually assimilated and clashed with more recent African American and Hispanic migrants. Meanwhile, political culture changed. Reformers weakened party organizations. Interest in politics waned, and media advertising replaced personal campaigning in many places. Does an area's history mirror these trends?

A third style of local politics, reform, often appeared in opposition to party organizations. While reform often had big business support, it also attracted small business and professionals, white-collar workers, and women. Reform frequently had a strong Protestant flavor, though it also drew upwardly mobile Catholics and Jews. Finally, reformers were strongest in middle- and upper-income neighborhoods, often on the outskirts of cities.

Reformers wanted cheap, honest, and efficient government. They emphasized issues and valued principles above personal relations. Reformers revamped city charters to have small councils elected at large (citywide), not from districts. They favored the "short ballot," in which fewer offices would be elected and more appointed. Some reform charters combined legislative and executive functions in city commissions, in which a small body of elected commissioners each ran a city department. Reformers disagreed about mayoral powers. Some called for a "strong mayor," with veto and appointment powers. More, however, preferred the "weak mayor"-city manager system. Here an appointed, supposedly nonpolitical, full-time administrator ran local government. Reformers modernized fiscal management and required competitive bidding for contracts to curb corruption.

To roll back political party organizations, reformers often made local elections nonpartisan and held them at different times from state and national elections. They tightened voter registration and election procedures to curb cheating. Reformers replaced patronage-based hiring with civil service, ended required political donations and campaigning by public employees, and often restricted their political activity.

Reformers changed more than government and politics. Moral reformers tried to suppress liquor, prostitution, gambling, certain sporting events, some movies and plays, and sexually oriented publications. Reformers also transformed schools, courts, welfare, recreation, and public health. Much of this activity involved government, either as a service provider or as a regulator of private conduct.

Many historians select a single issue, election, organization, or leader to explore reform politics in a community. It can be fruitful to

Women reformers, Chicago, n.d. Reformers were certain that people were rational and, if well-informed, would do the right thing (i.e., support reform). This photograph documents the important part women played in many reform groups. *Chicago Historical Society, Henry Delorval Green Papers, Box 13.*

compare the previous discussions with local experience. What conditions ignited the fires of reform? What ideas and plans did reformers advocate? What were their underlying assumptions about politics and society? What tactics and appeals did reformers use? What resistance did they face? How successful were reformers? What explains their results? When reformers succeeded, who gained and what did they win? Who lost? How did reformers change the structure and conduct of local government? How did they change participation in and results of local politics? How long did reform prevail? If temporary, why was this and what ended reform? If long-lasting, was it still reform?

This last question suggests that for all their attraction, both the boss-machine and the reform models described here are stereotypes concealing as much as they reveal. Some organization politicians implemented reforms, like modernizing government, suppressing corruption, or expanding civil service. Tom Pendergast's new charter, for instance, brought city manager government to Kansas City. On the other hand, some businessmen and reformers acted like bosses. As political scientist Amy Bridges demonstrated, reformers who installed city-manager systems, nonpartisan elections, and at-large councils in the Southwest built political organizations that completely dominated their cities. Researchers should be wary of labels and skeptical of rhetoric from any political combatant, and they should judge people by what they did, not just by what they said.

Urban liberalism was a fourth local political style. It used government power to restrict business and improve housing, working conditions, and other facets of daily life. Urban liberals typically drew their strongest support from workers, immigrants, and racial minorities. Early urban liberals included ex-businessmen Toledo Mayor Samuel "Golden Rule" Jones (1897–1904) and Cleveland Mayor Tom Johnson (1901–1909). Both favored publicly owned utilities, low transit fares, higher corporate taxes, and more parks and other public services. So did socialists elected in hundreds of cities. Milwaukee socialists improved workplace safety, parks, and playgrounds, and gave public employees higher pay and an eight-hour day. They also wanted municipal ownership of mass transit and electric companies, public food marketing and banking, and nonprofit housing, but opponents blocked most of this agenda. In many respects, urban liberals were like organization politicians. They differed, however, in stressing issues and policy changes, in making government more efficient, and in minimizing corruption.

During the Great Depression of the 1930s, a new generation of urban liberals updated what Jones, Johnson, and the socialists had done. Like "bosses," they practiced patronage politics and built strong precinct-level organizations. At the same time, they used government authority to change peoples' lives through work relief, public-sector construction, and public housing, mainly with federal money. Detroit Mayor Frank Murphy gave food and shelter to the jobless, pushed for lower utility rates and transit fares, and lobbied for federal aid to cities by helping to launch the U.S. Conference of Mayors.

ॐ ॐ ॐ ॐ ॐ

FIORELLO LA GUARDIA: URBAN LIBERALISM IN THE BIG APPLE

Fiorello La Guardia was an unusual politician. Raised on the Arizona frontier, he became the mayor of the largest city in the United

States from 1933 to 1945. A Republican in a largely Democratic city, he earned the distrust of party leaders and the confidence of voters regardless of party. Insisting on honest, impartial government, La Guardia was the first reform mayor of New York City to be reelected. Unlike many reformers, he was an ambitious, colorful self-promoter who raced to blazes in full firefighter gear and read comics over the radio during a newspaper strike. In his biography of La Guardia, historian Ronald Bayor used manuscript collections from city archives, the New York Public Library, and college and university depositories; oral histories collected at Columbia University; published memoirs; and scholarly dissertations, articles, and books.

Bayor describes three aspects of "The Little Flower's" liberalism. First, he cultivated support from new minorities (especially Italians, Jews, and blacks) by giving them government jobs and political prominence. Second, he ran an activist government that went to bat for common people. He increased relief for the jobless; built public housing, hospitals, and health clinics; started a health insurance plan for the poor; and used the threat of municipally owned electricity to push private utility rates down. Third, La Guardia, like Frank Murphy, pioneered in linking the U.S. government to the cities. A supporter of Franklin Roosevelt, La Guardia obtained big federal grants for highways, bridges, tunnels, parks, subways, a new sewage treatment system, and New York's first municipal airport, named after the mayor. Though La Guardia died in 1947 without fulfilling ambitions for higher political office, his record as the biggest U.S. city's longest-serving chief executive is no small monument.

Source: Ronald H. Bayor, *Fiorello La Guardia: Ethnicity and Reform* (Arlington Heights, IL: Harlan Davidson, 1993).

༃ ༃ ༃ ༃ ༃

Historians can research the history of urban liberals in any locality. What were the backgrounds of such politicians? Who supported them? What policies did they favor or enact? How much did they accomplish? Were urban liberals reformers? Or were they organization politicians? How useful are these labels? Even in times when historians claim liberals flourished like the 1930s and 1960s, they were not wholly successful. For example, during the Great Depression, Memphis took federal money for relief, public works, and public power. The New Deal gave Memphis public housing, parks, bridges, sewers, a hospital and zoo, airport and stadium, and Riverside Drive along the Mississippi River. But Memphis officials maintained their low-tax, small-government principles, were miserly toward the needy, and suppressed unions and African Americans. Did innovation or tradition characterize a community's politics during the 1930s or 1960s? What was the impact of national trends on local politics?

As the case of Memphis illustrates, in many places residents resisted change and outsiders. In the 1920s, for instance, the Ku Klux Klan flourished in the United States. Historian Kenneth Jackson attributed urban Klan strength in large part to white Protestants' fears that blacks and ethnic Catholics would capture their neighborhoods. More recent scholars also documented Klan racial, ethnic, and religious bigotry but add that such views were common outside the KKK. New work on the Klan emphasizes its defense of traditional morality, opposition to crime and liquor, and resistance to financial corruption and domination by the few. Did the KKK exist in a local community? If so, does its history parallel the discussion here?

༄༅ ༄༅ ༄༅ ༄༅ ༄༅

THE KU KLUX KLAN IN 1920s SMALL-TOWN AMERICA

Sandwiched between the Blue and Wallowa Mountains in northeastern Oregon, La Grande was a typical small town in the 1920s. Nearly all its 7,000 people were native-born whites, divided among Protestants, Mormons, and Roman Catholics. Forty-six Chinese and fifteen African Americans lived there, too. Like hundreds of other towns, La Grande was a service center for nearby farmers and loggers. It also was a railroad town, hosting repair shops for the Union Pacific.

Like many other communities, La Grande had a Ku Klux Klan chapter in 1922–1923, and historian David A. Horowitz has brought the klavern to light. To do so, he relied mainly on local KKK minutes at the Oregon Historical Center in Portland. In addition, Horowitz used city directories, census data, and newspapers and other periodicals to describe the La Grande Klan.

Early historians of the Klan had a national focus. But Horowitz and other recent scholars examined the KKK in local settings. According to Horowitz, the Klan was not the voice of the outcasts and the alienated. Rather, the group drew people from many walks of life, particularly mid- and low-level white collar and skilled workers. Local Klan leaders were merchants and professionals but not the town's richest and most powerful. In the Klan, members found fellowship, mutual support in business and politics, and a way to take part in the community.

During its brief history, the La Grande klavern entered local politics. It convinced the Board of Education to fire a Catholic teacher and won both school board seats in the June, 1922, election. A Klansman was then hired as school board clerk. The La Grande klavern, however, left less of a mark on the rest of local government. It supported candidates in the November 1922 city and state elections, but they all lost, some narrowly. Acting as a pressure group, the Klan defended La Grande's city manager (who gratefully joined) against press criticism, tried to win public jobs for members, and lobbied futilely for a better water system. The La Grande klavern devoted most of its attention, however, to agitating against crime, especially the production and sale of liquor.

Ardent opposition, factionalism, and sex scandal doomed the Klan in Oregon, as it did elsewhere. For a time, however, the KKK was a forum for "plain people" resisting unwanted change.

Source: David A. Horowitz, "Order, Solidarity, and Vigilance: The Ku Klux Klan in La Grande, Oregon," in Shawn Lay, ed., *The Invisible Empire in the West: Toward a New Historical Appraisal of the Ku Klux Klan in the 1920s* (Urbana: University of Illinois Press, 1992), pp. 185–215.

ఞఞఞఞఞ

Since World War II, racial change and conflict have stimulated many grass-roots defensive movements. In his study of Detroit in the 1940s, 1950s, and 1960s, historian Thomas Sugrue highlights the key role of white homeowners' groups. Detroit homeowners three times helped elect Mayor Albert Cobo (1950–1957), a Republican in a mainly Democratic city. They also put Thomas Poindexter, the "Home Owners' Champion," on the city council in 1964. Detroit homeowners' associations got Cobo to block a racially integrated housing cooperative and in 1964 convinced voters to pass a Homeowners' Rights Ordinance. Other U.S. cities in the post–World War II era replicated the politics of Detroit's neighborhood associations.

The civil rights movement's legal victories in the 1960s only heightened some whites' resistance to racial change. In the 1970s, whites of modest means protested court-ordered pupil busing to integrate public schools. Louise Day Hicks, Elvira "Pixie" Palladino, John Kerrigan, and others from South Boston, East Boston, and Charlestown shook Boston's school and municipal politics. What historian Ronald Formisano termed "reactionary populism" echoed earlier cries of Detroit homeowners. These white residents in both Boston and Detroit defended home and neighborhood, feared crime, felt insecure and powerless, and resented affluent suburbanites who avoided racial conflict by moving outside the city. Has a nearby community experienced

Antibusing demonstration, Detroit, 1975. Antibusing movements in the 1970s combined fierce defense of neighborhood with hostility toward blacks, the wealthy, and government. Busing was one issue moving white working-class voters from New Deal liberalism to a surging conservative Republican Party. *Carmen A. Roberts Papers, Box 1, Bentley Historical Library, University of Michigan.*

similar political turmoil? What sparked such reaction? How important were neighborhood, class, gender, religion, and ethnicity in these events? How did these movements shape local politics? How did they affect public policy? Were the effects temporary or long-lasting? How did the targets of such resistance respond?

Most grass-roots defensive movements, however, had nothing to do with race. Residents mobilized again and again to resist threats to homes and neighborhoods. Homes are not only people's largest financial assets but also confer status, identity, security, and quiet pleasures of life. It would be interesting to look into one or more such episodes in an area's past. Have residents organized against speeding or noisy traffic? Against plans to widen streets, build new highways, or install entrance-exit ramps? What land-use issues have touched off local outrage? Proposed apartments in single-family zones? Retail stores, with their traffic and noise, in or near residential areas? Have moral threats, like liquor sales, "adult" businesses, or prostitution prompted citizen action? Rising aesthetic and environmental concerns caused criticism of cellular telephone transmission towers, landfills, and industrial water or air pollution. What tactics did local residents use in these disputes? How successful were they? How does one account for the results? Quality of life politics was usually localized and short-lived, and often local news media gave it little or no coverage. Histori-

In 1952, women in a new outlying neighborhood of Chicago blocked traffic to dramatize their demand that the city pave their dusty street. *Chicago Historical Society, Photo Files, DN-0-5782.*

ans therefore tend to overlook the politics of neighborhood defense. Those who do not can produce fine local history.

A variation on business-dominated politics reshaped cities during the past half-century. Big business led the politics of urban redevelopment, but others joined as well. After World War II, well-off residents and much retail business and manufacturing moved from older cities to suburbs. As city tax bases declined, public service costs rose, especially as poor minorities replaced upper- and middle-income people. Real estate interests, property developers, banks and insurance firms, and major retailers vowed to halt urban economic decline. These business leaders enlisted urban liberals favoring slum clearance and public housing, construction unions and planners wanting large building projects, and professional politicians concerned about their city's image and their own reputations. Together they created what political scientist John Mollenkopf called "pro-growth coalitions."

ॐ ॐ ॐ ॐ ॐ

A PRO-GROWTH COALITION REMAKES THE CITY BY THE BAY

In *The Contested City*, a commentary on federal urban policy since the 1930s, political scientist John Mollenkopf used San Francisco to describe urban redevelopment politics. Mollenkopf's principal sources for this case study were government documents, journalists' accounts, and a biography of Mayor George Christopher.

After World War II, San Francisco business leaders watched uneasily as the Bay area's most powerful engines of economic growth left the city. These corporate chiefs believed that attracting business and tourists to downtown would revive San Francisco's economy. The racially mixed Western Addition, located near the central business district, became a redevelopment site.

Working through private groups like the Bay Area Council (1946) and the Blyth-Zellerbach Committee (1955), businessmen in 1959 persuaded Mayor Christopher to hire a forceful urban planner, M. Justin Herman, to head the San Francisco Redevelopment Agency. Under Herman, the SFRA destroyed two-thirds of Western Addition's housing, displacing 8,000 people. For every three housing units demolished, only two new ones were built. And one-third of the new housing cost too much for Western Addition's previous inhabitants; it went to middle- and upper-class renters whom planners wanted downtown. Herman limited neighborhood opposition by promising to help relocate residents and businesses and by concealing plans to cut the supply of affordable housing.

Building demolition to make way for urban renewal, Chicago, 1959. Federally funded urban renewal transformed the appearance and land usage in cities in the 1950s and 1960s, making winners and losers of many residents, executives, and investors. *Chicago Historical Society, Photo Files, ICHi-17210, Clarence W. Hines photograph.*

SFRA brought other major projects to the city's core, such as the Yerba Buena Convention Center, the Golden Gateway project (luxury apartments, corporate office buildings, and a Hyatt Regency Hotel), a Holiday Inn in Chinatown, and an industrial park at China Basin near Hunter's Point. By the 1970s, planners had transformed "blighted" areas near downtown, making the city by the bay more attractive to local business, conventions, and tourists.

Source; John H. Mollenkopf, *The Contested City* (Princeton, NJ: Princeton University Press, 1983).

ॐ ॐ ॐ ॐ ॐ

Local historians can trace urban redevelopment in their own communities in the decades after World War II. Who paid for these projects? Private capital? State or local government? The federal government, under the 1949 Housing Act and later legislation? Who decided what to destroy, what to build, and what locations to use? What sites did they choose? Why did they choose these places? What had occupied this land, and what happened to those people, churches, and businesses? Describe the land acquisition and demolition process. Was this land developed or did it remain vacant? If developed, what was built? In large cities, highways, sports arenas, office towers, hotels, civic and convention centers, universities, and hospitals most commonly occupied urban renewal sites. How did urban redevelopment benefit the community? What were its disadvantages? Who gained and who lost? To what degree did these endeavors fulfill their goals?

While pro-growth coalitions transformed central cities, another kind of politics emerged in the suburbs. By the 1970s, more people lived in suburbs than anywhere else; by the 1990s, their residents made the difference in national elections. Many suburbs fit the stereotype of affluent, mainly white, auto-based, low-density communities of single-family homes. But suburbs had apartments as well as detached homes; working-class and poor people as well as the affluent; and growing numbers of African Americans, Hispanics, and Asians. Suburbs ranged from older, crowded, decaying communities near central cities to luxurious estates thirty miles away. Nor were suburbs exclusively residential. They had smokestack industry, and they dominated emerging technology and information businesses. Meanwhile, suburban shopping strips, local malls, and huge enclosed regional shopping centers captured a majority of retail sales in most metropolitan regions. By the 1970s and 1980s, suburbs were economically and culturally independent of central cities.

Students of suburban political history will find it useful to ask whether political styles mentioned in this chapter apply to their towns. Some, citing suburban diversity, deny that a distinctive suburban political style exists. Others claim suburban and city politics do differ. They say suburbanites disliked partisanship and lacked strong party organizations in local elections. Slates of candidates campaigned in suburbs, but the Taxpayer Party or Citizens' Caucus was usually separate from Republicans or Democrats. Second, some say suburban voters were more likely to split their tickets between major party candidates in county, state, and national elections. Third, suburbanites allegedly disapproved of full-time politicians and expected officials to act for the common good, not for personal gain. Suburbanites hoped voters would decide things by being well-informed and rational. Consensus would emerge and the public interest would prevail. Suburban elections were, in fact, often uncontested. This model of suburban politics imitates urban reform. To what degree did it fit a particular suburb? If not, why? If so, why did suburbanites accept these values? Were suburbanites' views different from those of central city voters? Have these "suburban" values shaped national politics? Or were such values part of national political culture which influenced most localities?

Who shaped suburban politics? Perhaps the models of political power at the beginning of this chapter help answer this question. Although the informed, involved citizen was the ideal, few suburbanites were active in civic affairs. Busy with jobs and family, dual wage-earner household members concentrated on their private lives. Moreover, most suburbanites worked in another community, so their interest in where they lived was not intense. And as government became more complex and technical, even those who cared about it felt estranged from city hall. Therefore, suburban politics became the concern of a few.

One influential group consisted of retailers, professionals, and real estate agents who lived and worked in the same suburb. They met for breakfast at Main Street coffee shops. They mingled at Chamber of Commerce meetings and at Kiwanis, Rotary, or Optimists luncheons. They tended to favor low-cost government, low property taxes, and independence from their region's central city. Finally, at least until the 1980s, they favored economic growth that would expand the tax base and bring them more business.

Women's networks were also influential in suburban politics. Mothers of young children met at the local park, at parent-teacher associations, and through child care groups. Older women traded news at League of Women Voters forums, church fairs and study groups, charitable organizations, and at meetings of the garden club or Business and Professional Women. Women tended to support good public services, like schools, libraries, and recreation, and were willing to campaign for them. Women were also more likely than men to respond to environmental and ethical appeals.

Public employees were a third significant political force in suburbs. Both hourly and supervisory personnel favored more and better public services. With political parties enfeebled and most residents uninvolved, city managers and other appointed officials frequently set local agendas. They benefited from their claims of nonpartisanship and from their information and technical knowledge. Often, unelected city managers and county administrators became politically powerful, cultivating citizen support and guiding elected officials. How important were each of these three elements in your suburb? What other groups and individuals were significant in winning elections and making policy?

One would also do well to identify important political issues in a suburb. Were such matters distinctively "suburban" or items that could arise in any type of community? Did choices between autonomy and centralization, between small accessible government and big remote bureaucracy, fill local agendas? What form did such issues take? Describe and explain how residents made their decisions. Next, were taxes a big issue in a suburb? Antitax movements erupted in the late 1970s after inflation and strong housing demand drove up assessments and property taxes. Third, did the suburb have antigrowth politics? By the 1980s, many suburbs became so densely settled that their buildings and traffic jams made them seem like central cities. Greater environmental awareness also fueled antigrowth feeling. Did growth wars involve zoning? Would new development be residential, commercial, or industrial? If residential, single-family or multiunit housing? If single-family, what minimum lot sizes would a municipality require? Did growth battles center around building codes? Did they swirl around decisions to expand water and sewer lines to permit new development? Or over annexation or incorporation of new municipalities? Where were local growth wars fought? At zoning and planning commission meetings? Or at the ballot box? For example, in 1988, Orange County, California, ballot Measure A sought to halt new construction that worsened traffic congestion. After developers opposing Measure A outspent proponents $1.6 million to $48,000, voters rejected A 56 to 44 percent.

While many suburban residents fought growth, racial minorities looked to government for more, not less. As previously noted, minority politics began when European ethnics used political parties and government to improve their lives. African Americans, Hispanics, and Asian Americans in the last third of the twentieth century did the same. First, minority populations grew considerably, becoming a numerical majority in many cities. Political influence followed numbers. Meanwhile, in the 1950s and 1960s, the civil rights movement mobilized African Americans. Did this occur in a nearby community and with what results? Did civil rights forces challenge local government? What impact did the movement have on partisan politics, campaigns,

Precinct captains supporting Chicagoan Arthur Mitchell, first African American Democrat elected to the U.S. House of Representatives in 1934. *Chicago Historical Society, ICHi-25390, Arthur W. Mitchell Papers, Box 1, Folder 2.*

and elections? Did blacks' local political role change? Did new leaders emerge? How did they differ from old ones?

In the wake of civil rights activism came greater minority participation in government. The 1965 U.S. Voting Rights Act broke down legal barriers to voting and office holding, especially in the South and Southwest. When did blacks, Hispanics, or Asians get the right to vote and hold government positions in a community? How did this occur? What was the extent of minority voting and office holding? As early as 1967, mayoral victories by Richard Hatcher in Gary, Indiana, and Carl Stokes in Cleveland signaled the rise of minority politicians. In the South, newly empowered African American voters elected mayors Maynard Jackson in Atlanta (1973), Ernest "Dutch" Morial in New Orleans (1977), and Richard Arrington in Birmingham (1980). By 1983, the second, third, and fourth largest cities in the United States (Chicago,

Los Angeles, and Philadelphia) each had a black mayor. Though less publicized, black councilmembers and other local elected officials also increased substantially.

Other minorities also gained influence in city halls and county buildings. Hispanic populations grew even faster than blacks, owing to immigration and high birth rates. Demographers predicted that Hispanics would become the largest minority in the United States by the early twenty-first century. Previously slow to become citizens and to vote, Hispanics in the 1980s and 1990s registered and voted readily, motivated by heightened anti–immigrant agitation. From Miami to Denver, from Chicago to southern California, Hispanic candidates won public office. Hispanics won half of San Antonio's ten council posts in 1977 after a court switched council elections from citywide to district-based. Four years later, voters there chose Henry Cisneros mayor; he later served in President Bill Clinton's cabinet.

Other minorities also made local political gains. Since the 1960s, substantial immigration to the United States and Canada from East Asia helped elect Asian-Americans to public office, especially on the West Coast. Following the lead of racial minorities, openly gay and lesbian candidates won local election campaigns. Although not a numerical minority, women had been traditionally underrepresented in politics and government. During the last three decades of the twentieth century, this began to change. Female voters now strongly supported female candidates. Women's image of honesty and nonpartisanship also appealed to voters disgusted with traditional politics. As with racial minorities, women made their greatest gains in school board, municipal, township, and county elections. Though mass media and scholars focused on minority politics in big cities, women, Asians, Hispanics, and African Americans often attained their greatest triumphs in small cities. For example, Cubans won more complete control over Hialeah, Florida, than in better-known Miami.

The study of a racial minority prominent in a community's politics can be revealing. What similarities to and differences from the experiences of European immigrants does one find? For towns with more than one large minority, it is possible to compare their political histories. Researchers can also explore political relations between or among different minorities in a locality. What conflict or cooperation occurred? At the same time, it is interesting to observe and explain internal rifts within each minority. Were such conflicts based on social class, beliefs, point of origin, color, age, or time of arrival? Although minority groups try to appear unified to outsiders, internal differences tend to grow as a group's numbers rise.

Uncovering the History of Urban Politics

Historians of minority politics may select one facet or may attempt comprehensive coverage. Voting behavior is a part of the story. How did voter turnout of a specific group compare to the community as a whole? What partisan preferences or other voting patterns appeared? Researchers can answer such questions by choosing several elections that will yield useful data. To document voting behavior in high-minority areas, match precinct or district-level election returns with census data. Public voter records make it possible to measure turnout. For some times and places, political survey data may be available. After finding the results, it is still necessary to explain them.

A second path leads to minority political organizations and activities. What minority pressure groups existed in an area? Describe their goals and membership. What did they do? What issues did they pursue? What tactics did they use? Measure and explain their success.

Some prefer to study minority candidates for public office. Did local party organizations exclude or recruit minority candidates? Who were the minority candidates? Were they representative of their group? What barriers or advantages did they encounter raising campaign funds? In what sort of districts did they run? Where their group had a majority? In multiethnic or multiracial districts? How did they appeal to voters of their own group? Harold Washington captured Chicago city hall in 1983 with the slogan "It's Our Turn" and a huge African American turnout. This typified a "first wave" of minority candidates who stirred group pride and overcame fierce opposition. In 1973, for example, Michigan State Senator Coleman Young became Detroit's first African American mayor by winning 92 percent of the black vote, defeating Roman Gribbs who won 91 percent of the whites. In polarized elections, who crossed group lines and why? What success did racial minority candidates have winning white voters or women hopefuls getting male support? What appeals did such candidates use? When minority politicians built coalitions, who were their partners? Other minorities? Working-class whites? Upper-status whites? In many places, a "second wave" of minority candidates forged multiracial alliances, and voter polarization declined.

A fourth possibility is to trace minorities' impact on local government. Where blacks, Hispanics, gays, or women won, what difference did it make? How did minority office-holders define themselves? As black or Asian county commissioners or as county commissioners who were black or Asian? Did racial and governmental roles conflict? If so, how did officials resolve the dilemma? What priorities did minority officials in a city have? Did they emphasize better parks, street repair, garbage collection, and other public services for their own group? Did they try to increase minority public employment, especially in positions in which it was scarce? Coleman Young, for instance, doubled blacks' share of Detroit's administrative jobs from 12 to 24 percent in four years. Did minority politicians give more public contracts to minority-owned businesses? Under Mayor Roy West, Richmond, Virginia, required city contractors to award minority subcontractors 30 percent of the dollar amount of their business. (The U.S. Supreme Court ended this policy in 1989.) What other goals have minority officials sought? Before federal civil rights legislation, some pressed for local antidiscrimination ordinances. Gays and lesbians, unprotected by federal law, still do. Finally, when minority officials did not have an agenda of advancing group interests, how did the public react?

༺ ༺ ༺ ༺ ༺

BLACK POWER IN THE CAPITAL OF THE NEW SOUTH

Atlanta during the mayoral terms of Maynard Jackson (1973–1981, 1989–1993) and Andrew Young (1981–1989) illustrates the achievements and limits of minority politics. Would black power help the black middle class? The black masses? Could minority public officials satisfy both their voters and corporate leaders?

By 1973, Atlanta was at a turning point. White suburbanization and black population growth had given African Americans a majority. Sam Massell, a Jewish liberal, had won with black support but was facing a reelection challenge from Vice-Mayor Maynard Jackson, a forceful, articulate thirty-five-year-old black attorney. Jackson had won his job despite older African American leaders' preference for a more seasoned and more diplomatic candidate. Jackson thus not only represented rising black political power but a new generation of minority leadership.

Jackson's boldness paid off in 1973. Although Massell courted white voters with the slogan "Atlanta's Too Young To Die," enough of them chose Jackson to give Atlanta's first black mayor nearly three-fifths of the total in a run-off election. Jackson won 95 percent of the blacks and 17 percent of the whites. At the same time, a change from at-large to district-based elections allowed African Americans to take nine of eighteen council seats.

As Jackson later recalled, on entering office he faced "exaggerated white anxiety and . . . exaggerated black expectations." Minority hiring and promotions were high priorities for Jackson. Blacks' share of city jobs rose from 42 to 56 percent in his first term. The biggest gains occurred in managerial (minority ranks up from 14 to 33 percent, 1972–1978) and professional positions (from 19 to 42, 1973–1978). Police and fire departments also became more diverse, despite fierce resistance. To meet his goals, Jackson imposed a city residency requirement and gave less weight to standardized tests. And the U.S. Congress helped by extending bans on job discrimination to state and local government.

Jackson also vowed to make black Atlanta more prosperous by giving more city contracts to minority-owned firms. In his first term, the percentage of city dollars spent with minority contractors jumped from 2 to 33. Furthermore, firms doing business with the city had to hire minority workers. Construction of MARTA, the mass transit network, and of Hartsfield Airport, both funded mainly from Washington, enabled Jackson to fulfill his pledges.

Jackson, however, was less successful convincing the private sector to include more African Americans. Jackson threatened to pull city funds out of major banks unless they added black and female board members and improved minority hiring. Confrontation, though, produced only minor progress.

Jackson also sympathized with neighborhoods resisting expressways and other massive development, a matter that cut across racial lines. Backing away from large-scale demolition and construction, Jackson created a Division of Neighborhood Planning and created Neighborhood Planning Units which had a voice in planning and zoning.

Although black Atlanta backed Jackson overwhelmingly, it was not entirely satisfied with what happened after elections. The biggest gains from Jackson's hiring and contracting policies went to African American business people, professionals, and the middle class. In the city, private employment for unskilled labor and factory workers continued to shrink, and city government could not reverse this trend. Jobs abounded in the fast-growing northern suburbs. But few blacks lived there, and suburbanites rejected mass transit which would have made jobs accessible to people without cars.

White corporate leaders were also displeased, since they had lost their political dominance at city hall and their previous partnership with nonconfrontational black spokesmen. Jackson did not consult big business and sometimes even denounced it publicly. The *Atlanta Constitution* retaliated by criticizing the mayor's performance and printing stories on "a city in crisis."

After a racially polarized second-term victory in 1977, Jackson and downtown business each realized they needed the other. Jackson began holding Pound Cake Summits, private meetings with corporate executives. The mayor also established the Atlanta Economic Development Corporation, a public-private business growth agency. He backed a hotel tax for convention/tourism promotion and eased minority subcontracting requirements for airport construction. Significantly, when garbage workers struck in 1977, Jackson, who had joined their strike parade in 1970, threatened to fire them unless they returned to work.

Conciliation of corporate Atlanta accelerated under Jackson's successor, Andrew Young, former aide to Martin Luther King, Jr. and former ambassador to the United Nations. Young often met with business executives and traveled to recruit business to Atlanta. He did little for the black underclass, abolished the Neighborhood Planning Division, and ended the NPU's staff support. Young used $6 million in federal low-income housing funds to revive Underground Atlanta, an entertainment-tourist district. Nearby, the city planned a domed stadium and upper-income housing. Young backed a new east side expressway, the Presidential Parkway, and a truck-rail freight yard, despite vocal neighborhood protest. And he vetoed a preservation plan for Midtown, which faced intensive development pressure.

With their ballots, Atlanta voters secured "black power." But some enjoyed it more than others. Though middle-class African Americans prospered from public policies, the poor remained in a world apart. After a brief intermission, big business again found friendly smiles at city hall. And after high hopes, neighborhoods could not count on city government to protect them from development. When he retired in 1989, Andrew Young declared that Atlanta had "sent a message to the world that we know how to do business."

Sources: Ronald H. Bayor, *Race and the Shaping of Twentieth-Century Atlanta* (Chapel Hill: University of North Carolina Press, 1996), and Clarence N. Stone, *Regime Politics: Governing Atlanta, 1946–1988* (Lawrence: University Press of Kansas, 1989).

꒰ꇵ꒱꒰ꇵ꒱꒰ꇵ꒱꒰ꇵ꒱꒰ꇵ꒱

Since the late 1960s, American voters have become increasingly conservative. This was apparent in U.S. presidential elections and with Republicans winning control of first the Senate and then the House of Representatives. Both major parties moved to the right. Conservatives tried to cut the size and power of government and transfer public functions to the private sector. They wanted less taxation, business regulation, welfare, and union power. They gave tax breaks to business to spur economic growth and hoped government would defend traditional moral standards.

Not surprisingly, conservatives left their mark on local politics and government, too. One can examine the impact of conservative strength in a community. Perhaps existing groups turned right, and maybe new organizations entered local politics. For example, did evangelical Christians take part in city or county politics? What was the relationship between new forces on the right and established parties and interest groups? Next, what issues did conservatives raise in local politics? Did they initiate things or block what others proposed? How did the community respond? Did conservatives change the political process? That is, did they introduce new ways to lobby or to campaign? Did they change government, such as imposing term limits on office holders? How successful were conservatives? One might judge and explain the typicality of a single community's experience.

༃༃༃༃༃

LOS ANGELES ELECTS A CONSERVATIVE MAYOR

In 1993–1994, the two largest U.S. cities elected Republican mayors, a clear sign of conservative domination of American politics. The story of one of these men, Richard Riordan of Los Angeles, illustrates both the appeal and limits of conservatism at the local level.

When Democrat Tom Bradley, the city's first African American mayor, retired after twenty years in office, Los Angeles faced big problems. Besides traffic, air pollution, wildfires, and earthquakes, Los Angeles had a weak economy and strong racial tensions, as the police beating of Rodney King and subsequent rioting showed. Michael Woo, a city councilmember backed by white liberals, Asians, and blacks, hoped to succeed Bradley. His leading opponent was Richard Riordan, a wealthy investor and corporate deal maker. Riordan ran as a nonpolitical businessman, who would restore prosperity, shrink government, and suppress crime by adding 3,000 new police officers. Riordan declared himself "tough enough to turn L.A. around." With three million dollars of his own fortune and with money from media owner Rupert Murdoch, Riordan defeated Woo on June 8, 1993. A conservative would now sit in the mayor's chair.

As mayor, Riordan fulfilled many of his goals. He claimed that he hired 2,000 more police officers in his first term and that crime plunged. The economy recovered, and Riordan took credit for 30,000 new jobs. He cut taxes, improved efficiency, and balanced the budget, wiping out a $200 million deficit. Riordan convinced voters to increase mayoral authority to dismiss department heads with council approval. He also sounded other conservative themes. He criticized environmental controls on land use and air quality. He also favored decentralizing the public schools, something white suburbanites and some African Americans found congenial.

But as conservatives in Washington also discovered, political realities limit change. Riordan's conservatism had its boundaries. Los Angeles is racially and culturally diverse, and the new mayor avoided issues that energized conservatives elsewhere. He showed little enthusiasm for fighting abortion or gay/lesbian rights. Since Hispanics were two-fifths of his city's population and had given him about half of their votes, Riordan sat out the anti-immigration crusade of some California Republicans. Though a Republican, Riordan maintained ties to Democrats. Before running for mayor, he had helped finance Bradley's campaigns and had served as Bradley's parks and recreation commission president. As mayor, Riordan continued to court Democrats, endorsing Democratic U.S. Senator Diane Feinstein for reelection. Riordan also retreated from privatization efforts after city council and city employees balked. Disillusioned Republicans wore RINO buttons—"Republican in Name Only."

Riordan's approach disappointed some conservatives but pleased most voters. In 1997, he easily won a second term, overwhelming State Senator Tom Hayden, a founder of Students for a Democratic Society and a Vietnam War opponent in the 1960s. In this campaign, Riordan won some Democratic support, including from Feinstein and the local AFL-CIO. He also benefited from low turnout among poor and minority residents whom Hayden did not inspire.

This brief case study relies on recent periodicals. Both *Readers' Guide to Periodical Literature* and on-line computer databases such as CITE provide references for Riordan and for Los Angeles. These indexes led to articles in newsmagazines such as *Newsweek, Time,* and *Business Week;* journals of opinion such as *New Republic* and *National Review;* and a local publication, *Los Angeles* magazine. In addition, the *New York Times,* which also has its own index, reported on Riordan. One can also consult the daily *Los Angeles Times,* which some libraries own and others can borrow through interlibrary loan. While reading press sources, notice differences and similarities. To what extent do they repeat the same themes? What distinguishes one source from another? What aspects of the story do they cover the most? What do they tend to omit? Where could one obtain evidence these accounts leave out?

To create an accurate, perceptive, and lively sense of the past, a historian will want to find a variety of sources and use them skillfully. Chapter 2 contained some advice about these tasks. As noted there, written sources include both public evidence, like newspapers, magazines, and government reports, and documents produced for private purposes, like diaries and letters. Some political organizations published newspapers or newsletters, which archives or libraries may have. Wise researchers do not limit themselves to local sources, since national magazines and newspapers often cover politics in specific communities. Perhaps local citizens have kept collections of campaign materials. If possible, supplement written evidence by talking to people with first-hand knowledge. It is fruitful to speak with ordinary residents, not just officials and politicians. Finally, as Chapter 2 advised, draw on election returns, election-day voter lists, voter registration records, original census lists and aggregate census data, city directories, and minutes of legislative bodies. These numerous sources, representing many viewpoints, are the raw materials for documenting the political history of local communities.

SUGGESTED READINGS

Floyd Hunter, *Community Power Structure* (Chapel Hill: University of North Carolina Press, 1953), and Robert Dahl, *Who Governs?* (New Haven, CT: Yale University Press, 1961), are classic studies by political scientists. For two historians' works, see Carl V. Harris, *Political Power in Birmingham, 1871–1921* (Knoxville: University of Tennessee Press, 1977), and David C. Hammack, *Power and Society: Greater New York at the Turn of the Century* (New York: Columbia University Press, 1982). For discussions of business dominance in Sunbelt cities, see essays in Richard M. Bernard and Bradley R. Rice, eds., *Sunbelt Cities: Politics and Growth Since World War II* (Austin: University of Texas Press, 1983).

For an introduction to boss and machine politics, begin with Alexander B. Callow, Jr., ed., *The City Boss in America* (New York: Oxford University Press, 1976). Callow also wrote *The Tweed Ring* (New York: Oxford University Press, 1966), which described a corrupt New York City machine. John M. Allswang offers brief descriptions in *Bosses, Machines, and Urban Voters* (revised ed., Baltimore: Johns Hopkins University Press, 1986). Book-length case studies of boss politics abound. Besides Callow on Tweed and Lyle W. Dorsett, *The Pendergast Machine* (New York: Oxford University Press, 1968), see Amy Bridges, *A City in the Republic: Antebellum New York and the Origins of Machine Politics*

(Ithaca, NY: Cornell University Press, 1984); Roger Biles, *Big City Boss in Depression and War: Mayor Edward J. Kelly of Chicago* (DeKalb: Northern Illinois University Press, 1984); Biles, *Richard J. Daley: Politics, Race, and the Governing of Chicago* (DeKalb: Northern Illinois University Press, 1995); and Zane L. Miller, *Boss Cox's Cincinnati: Urban Politics in the Progressive Era* (New York: Oxford University Press, 1968). For the story behind one widely read primary source on machine politics, see Terrence J. McDonald's introduction to William L. Riordan's *Plunkitt of Tammany Hall* (Boston: Bedford Books of St. Martin's Press, 1994). Two significant articles are Daniel Czitrom, "Underworlds and Underdogs: Big Tim Sullivan and Metropolitan Politics in New York, 1889–1913," *Journal of American History*, 78 (September, 1991), 536–558; and Harvey Boulay and Alan DiGaetano, "Why Did Political Machines Disappear?" *Journal of Urban History*, 12 (November, 1985), 25–49.

Reformers were less colorful than bosses, and so is the scholarship about them. In *The New City: Urban America in the Industrial Age, 1860–1920* (Arlington Heights, IL: Harlan Davidson, 1985), Raymond A. Mohl offers a brief overview of varieties of urban reform. Good monographs are Martin J. Schiesl, *The Politics of Efficiency: Municipal Administration and Reform in America, 1880–1920* (Berkeley: University of California Press, 1977); Bradley Rice, *Progressive Cities: The Commission Government Movement in America, 1901–1920* (Austin: University of Texas Press, 1977); and Kenneth Fox, *Better City Government: Innovation in American Urban Politics, 1850–1937* (Philadelphia: Temple University Press, 1977). Amy Bridges, *Morning Glories: Municipal Reform in the Southwest* (Princeton, NJ: Princeton University Press, 1997), covers the Sunbelt.

For urban liberalism, begin with Mohl, *The New City*. Bruce M. Stave, ed., *Socialism and the Cities* (Port Washington, NY: Kennikat Press, 1975), covers a half-dozen localities. Economic historian Douglas Booth assesses "Municipal Socialism and City Government Reform: The Milwaukee Experience, 1910–1940," in *Journal of Urban History*, 12 (November, 1985), 51–74. Several studies document politics in the 1930s. See Charles H. Trout, *Boston, The Great Depression, and the New Deal* (New York: Oxford University Press, 1977); Roger Biles, *Big City Boss in Depression and War*; Stave, *The New Deal and the Last Hurrah: Pittsburgh Machine Politics* (Pittsburgh: University of Pittsburgh Press, 1970); and Sidney Fine, *Frank Murphy: The Detroit Years* (Ann Arbor: University of Michigan Press, 1975). Some books emphasize the limited nature of political change in the 1930s. See, for example, Douglas L. Smith, *The New Deal in the Urban South* (Baton Rouge: Louisiana State University Press, 1988), Jo Ann E. Argersinger, *Toward a New*

Deal in Baltimore: People and Government in the Great Depression (Chapel Hill: University of North Carolina Press, 1988); and Roger Biles, *Memphis in the Great Depression* (Knoxville: University of Tennessee Press, 1986).

For the politics of grass-roots defensive movements, begin with Kenneth T. Jackson, *The Ku Klux Klan in the City: 1915-1930* (New York: Oxford University Press, 1967), which profiles major cities of the South, Midwest, and West. Current assessments of the Klan appear in Shawn Lay, ed., *The Invisible Empire in the West: Toward a New Historical Appraisal of the Ku Klux Klan of the 1920s* (Urbana: University of Illinois Press, 1992), and Lay, *Hooded Knights on the Niagara: The Ku Klux Klan in Buffalo, New York* (New York: New York University Press, 1995). An important study of postwar urban decline and race relations is Thomas J. Sugrue, *The Origins of the Urban Crisis: Race and Inequality in Postwar Detroit* (Princeton, NJ: Princeton University Press, 1996). Ronald P. Formisano, *Boston Against Busing: Race, Class, and Ethnicity in the 1960s and 1970s* (Chapel Hill: University of North Carolina Press, 1991), explores racial politics a generation later.

The definitive history of urban redevelopment is Jon C. Teaford, *The Rough Road to Renaissance: Urban Revitalization in America, 1940-1985* (Baltimore: Johns Hopkins University Press, 1990). Roy Lubove, *Twentieth Century Pittsburgh: Government, Business, and Environmental Change* (New York: Wiley, 1969), tells the story of an early urban redevelopment effort, while John H. Mollenkopf, *The Contested City* (Princeton, NJ: Princeton University Press, 1983), offers case studies of Boston and San Francisco.

The classic work on suburban politics was Robert C. Wood, *Suburbia: Its People and Their Politics* (Boston: Houghton Mifflin, 1958). A recent survey of suburban issues in Orange County, California, is Mark Baldassare, *Trouble in Paradise: The Suburban Transformation in America* (New York: Columbia University Press, 1986). In *Edge City: Life on the New Frontier* (New York: Doubleday, 1991), reporter Joel Garreau describes North America's newest urban form, and in *Post-Suburbia: Government and Politics in the Edge Cities* (Baltimore: Johns Hopkins University Press, 1997), historian Jon C. Teaford probes the shifting balance between growth and the suburban ideal.

Studies of racial minority politics are accumulating; most describe individual cities, politicians, and elections. William E. Nelson, Jr. and Philip J. Meranto, *Electing Black Mayors: Political Action in the Black Community* (Columbus: Ohio State University Press, 1977), covers the first wave of big-city black mayors, Richard Hatcher in Gary and Carl Stokes in Cleveland. Chicago's dynamic Mayor Harold Washington attracted several commentators. See Melvin G. Holli and Paul M. Green, eds., *The Making of the Mayor: Chicago 1983* (Grand Rapids, MI: William B. Eerdmans, 1984); Holli and Green, eds., *Bashing Chicago Traditions: Harold Washington's Last Campaign* (Grand Rapids, MI: William B. Eerdmans, 1989); and Gary Rivlin, *Fire on the Prairie: Chicago's Harold Washington and the Politics of Race* (New York: Henry Holt, 1992). Christopher Silver and John V. Moeser take a comparative approach to black politics in *The Separate City: Black Communities in the Urban South, 1940–1968* (Lexington: University Press of Kentucky, 1995). In *Politics in Black and White: Race and Power in Los Angeles* (Princeton, NJ: Princeton University Press, 1993), Raphael J. Sonenshein discusses biracial coalitions and factions.

Chapter 6

TRACING LOCAL CAMPAIGNS AND ELECTIONS

Campaigns and elections make ideal historical projects. They occur in short time periods, so one can research them efficiently. They are visible events, producing public records and news coverage. And they can be dramatic, with strategies and tactics, competition and suspense, and emotional highs and lows. In campaigns and elections, communities settle disputes and define what they are and want to be. Here is a guide to this important part of local history.

Historians choose the campaigns or elections to study according to what they want to accomplish. Those interested in the election process can select any example, providing that adequate sources remain. Campaigns are also ways historians learn more about their communities—their winning and losing candidates, political parties, social and political movements, neighborhoods, and population groups. Choosing specific elections in the past is also a good way of finding out how a locality dealt with challenges or conflicts. What impact did immigrants or rural migrants make on a single city? What changes occurred after the United Auto Workers organized the aircraft factory? How did a town's campaigns and elections reflect its evolution from semirural village to bustling suburb? Studying selected campaigns and elections may provide answers to questions like these.

A good way to begin is by introducing the audience to the context of politics of the community under study. Indicate the type of government, the elected offices at stake, jurisdictions from which candidates ran, terms of office, election dates, and other basic facts. What were the area's characteristics—its history, prominent personalities, customs, and people? Describe the locality's political patterns so readers will understand the significance of what they will subsequently learn.

HOW TO UNLOCK THE HISTORY OF LOCAL ELECTIONS

Many of the sources useful in revealing the history of campaigns and elections have been mentioned already. Books and articles by historians, contemporary newspapers and periodicals, clipping files at archives and newspaper offices, and census data each may be helpful. But some deserve special mention. Interviews bring the past to life and can yield evidence missing from printed sources. It is wise to talk not only to candidates and office-holders but also to campaign workers and to voters. Consult people of varying social backgrounds and viewpoints. Chapter 2 offered pointers and cited guidebooks about oral history.

Historians trace voting behavior through public records. Clerks' offices keep voter registration records, election-day poll lists, and precinct and district election totals. Matching them with census data uncovers voting rates and political preferences of various population groups. Link individual voter records and poll lists with city directories or census lists to learn more about who voted. Young or old? Long-time residents or newcomers? Rich or poor? Whites or racial minorities? How do findings about who voted explain the decisions local government made?

Political historians follow other leads as well. Since the 1970s and 1980s, U.S. and Canadian political campaigns have had to disclose contributions and expenditures, creating yet another historical source. City or county clerks or state/provincial offices keep such reports. Campaign artifacts, like flyers and handbills, buttons, door hangers, and posters identify campaign themes and tactics and help capture their flavor. Most people discard these items, but museums or archives may keep them. Moreover, individuals may save objects from campaigns they joined. Political parties and interest groups retain records, too. They don't have to show their files, but personal contacts can often open closed doors. Even availability of official records varies. Some local governments make it easy to examine election materials. In other places, you may have to quiz old-timers to learn their locations. Unfortunately, many governments misplaced or destroyed official records.

One approach to politics in a community is to study a group involved in local campaigns. In the past, political parties were the most important such organization. People were fiercely loyal to a party,

Tracing Local Campaigns and Elections   129

Cigar-smoking politicians plan for the next election, Macomb County, Michigan, 1960s or early 1970s. *Don Binkowski Papers, Box 10, Bentley Historical Library, University of Michigan.*

since one's allegiance stemmed from strong religious, ethnic, racial, and regional identities. Under the patronage system, people got jobs and other valuable benefits from party politics. Before television, politics occurred first-hand, not through media images. With fewer competing diversions, people argued about politics and enjoyed the spectacle of campaigns. How influential were political parties at various points in the past? How would one answer this question? Why have parties declined?

Historians examine political parties in several ways. Some compare Democrats and Republicans, Conservatives and Liberals, during a particular period. Others trace a single party over time to document change. You might want to describe the structure and organization of the Republican or Democratic party in your city, township, or county. What state laws governed parties? What did each party actually do? Did it recruit candidates for public office? If so, how and using what criteria? What support did it give candidates' campaigns? Information? Money? Volunteers? Or merely a network of contacts? How did the party get money and how did it spend it? What sort of people became party leaders? Did they also hold government positions? Why did they spend their time and effort on party politics? What types of voters did each party attract? Why? Did a party define itself through its positions on issues? If so, what were they? If not, why would residents support a particular party? Did the party try to shape public policy? If so, how and with what success? It can be a mistake to regard a political party as a unified group. The larger a party, the more likely it developed competing factions. The historian can probe the sources of these divisions. Did they stem from personality conflicts? Geographical differences? Disagreements about issues? Did party factions persist or mutate over time? Perhaps a community had third-party or minor-party movements. If not, why? If so, explain their appeal and assess their successes and failures.

As parties weakened, other groups gained political strength. Political scientists term them interest groups; opponents pejoratively call them pressure groups. Some, like Chambers of Commerce, downtown retailers' associations, or real estate boards, represented business interests. Others, such as the Farm Bureau, Grange, and National Farmers' Organization, spoke for agriculture. Perhaps an area had a local labor federation composed of individual unions, including public employees (American Federation of State, County, and Municipal Employees), building trades (plumbers, carpenters, and electricians) and industrial unions, like auto, steel, and rubber workers. Still other interest groups reflected ethnic, racial, or gender identities. Examples included the Polish Falcons, the National Association for the Advancement of Colored People, and the Women's Christian Temperance Union. Age (senior citizens clubs), residence (neighborhood associations), and religion also prompted common political action.

It can be enlightening to select one or more interest groups in a city or county. Who joined? What were the group's purposes or goals? What did it do in local politics? Did it make campaign endorsements and donations? If so, how did it decide? Did it make its preferences public or simply tell its members? Did it provide campaign workers? What difference did its campaign activity make? Which groups were most influential? How can one determine this? What was the relationship between interest groups and political parties? For example, in some places, organized labor and the Democratic Party were intertwined. Business groups and Republicans were often close partners.

Local historians also uncover the past by focusing on individual candidates. They may decide to learn about a specific politician. Or

Tracing Local Campaigns and Elections 131

they may find it more satisfying to do a group portrait. Researchers can choose one point in the past or trace historical change and continuity by selecting several different times. They compile candidate profiles by using city directories, census lists, clipping files, newspapers, and published local histories. Note age, race, gender, religion, education, occupation, length of residence, and prior community activity of those who ran for public office. Were they representative of the community? How did they differ from their neighbors? In partisan elections, did Democratic and Republican candidates differ or were they similar to each other?

Why did a given candidate seek public office? Did a political party or interest group recruit him or her? If so, what made that person attractive to their sponsors? Did candidates decide to run on their own? What were their motives? Belief in a particular issue? Partisan duty? Hostility to an opponent? Zest for combat? Personal ambition? Need for attention? Desire to compensate for failing at something else? What did they gain from running? What did they lose? Did their bids for public office hurt their jobs, families, and personal lives? What can one learn about why most people did not run for public office?

A local campaign history should specify how candidates got on the election ballot. In some cases, this occurred by nomination at a party convention. Under this system, party activists met at Democratic or Republican headquarters, a saloon, or other meeting hall to choose candidates. Did political parties or caucuses in a community use this system? How did it work? Who gained and who lost? If parties gave up nominating conventions, when and why did it happen?

In the twentieth century, reformers claimed the convention system was undemocratic and controlled by "party bosses." U.S. reformers replaced party conventions with primary elections, in which party members chose their nominees by majority vote. By the last third of the century, many states no longer limited voting in primaries to declared party supporters. Some permitted any voter to take part in "open primaries." An individual became a primary election candidate by obtaining signatures on nominating petitions. After being filed, these petitions became public documents retained by city or county clerks. Examining them will tell much about the petition process. What do the patterns of names, addresses, dates, and circulators reveal? In some jurisdictions, one could get on the ballot by paying a filing fee. Why did states adopt this method? Whom did it help?

Although many residents ignore primary elections, local historians should not. Where one political party dominates, primaries determine general election winners. Even with two-party competition, primaries can reveal much. They are not merely an earlier type of general election. Primaries have their own flavor. Since they pit members of the same party against each other, primaries can be as bitter as a family feud. Historians can learn much from writing the history of some local primary elections. Did intraparty divisions stem from personal ambitions or factions? Territorial interests? Conflicts about issues? Racial, religious, or ethnic fault lines? Did divisions remain after the primary or did the party unite? How did divisive primaries affect the ensuing general election?

Primary elections have other distinctive features. Few people vote in them, since interest in politics is low early in the election cycle. Others do not vote because they believe, correctly or not, they must declare party preference and don't want to do so. Thus, primary campaigns chase small numbers of potential voters, permitting a few well-organized, highly-motivated people to win. Although designed as intraparty contests, primaries did not always stay that way. They sometimes drew opposing party's supporters who had no primary of their own to "keep them home." Thus, Republicans could win primaries with Democratic support, and Republicans sometimes helped pick Democratic candidates.

If "third parties" (minor parties) appeared in a town, they raise questions about ballot access. Who decided how candidates got on general election ballots? What were the requirements? Was it easy or difficult? Did minor parties have to do different things to get on the ballot than Democrats or Republicans, Conservatives or Liberals? Did legal or political disputes over ballot access erupt? What were the results? Could a person run as an independent in a partisan election? In many Canadian and U.S. communities, local elections have been formally nonpartisan, with candidates not identified by party label. In these places, how did candidates get on the ballot?

Third parties also pose historical problems for the two-party system. Why did a minor party appear in a community? Did it reflect major party failure to address or solve an important issue? Or did the third party have little appeal? Was it merely a vehicle for personal ambition? How did Republicans or Democrats react to a minor party in a locality? Pretend it did not exist? Seek to undermine it by adopting some of its style or issues? Or attempt to suppress it? Did the third party fade away or become a major party?

An account of campaign organization is an essential part of any election history. Who ran the campaign? There may have been a campaign manager, office manager, treasurer, scheduler, or chairs for fundraising, publicity, events, and district organization. Who chose these people and what criteria did they use? Loyalty to candidate or party? Political experience? Personal skills, like reliability and judgment? Commitment of time to the campaign? Did campaign teams consist of volunteers, paid staff, or a combination of the two? Many campaigns were family affairs, with the candidate, spouse, children, or other relatives making decisions. Other teams consisted of the candidate and close friends. In still other cases, candidates depended on the group that sponsored them, be it a church, child care network, fraternal order, union, or business circle. Where political parties were strong, their organizations did the campaigning. What occurred in a specific area? Assess strengths and weaknesses of the campaign team under study.

Nearly all campaigns need money, and in general the more funds they have, the more likely they are to win. Unless a campaign filed public reports, however, it may be difficult to document revenue and spending. Nevertheless, one should try to do so using interviews, internal campaign records, and press accounts. Did the campaign have a budget? How did it set financial goals? How much money did it raise? How did this amount compare to its opponents? To other similar campaigns? From where did contributions come? Candidates and their families? Campaign team? Friends? Neighbors? Community residents who supported the candidate personally or favored the candidate's political party? Members of groups to which he or she belonged? Other interest groups in and out of the community? How much money came from the candidate's political party? From businesses, including current and would-be contractors with local government? From public employees? What proportion of funds came from outside the candidate's district or from outside the community? Explain such contributions. What patterns can one find in the sizes of contributions? How did the campaign raise funds? From individual contacts? Fundraising events? Why did contributors donate to campaigns? What did they hope to get for their money? To what degree did campaign donations reflect donor choice or coercion of contributors? By examining several campaigns, it is possible for researchers to identify patterns of who gave money and how much each contributed.

Students of local politics also trace campaign spending. What amount and proportion of money went for operations, like headquarters, office supplies and equipment, salaries, and food? How much did a campaign spend on contacting voters? Which methods of contacting voters cost a lot and which were inexpensive? In some cases, expense determines how campaigns contact voters, while other times candidates do what they believe to be easiest or most effective. Did campaigns benefit from donated time, office space, and materials? If so, how much? Did campaign spending seem thrifty or extravagant? Investigators can measure per capita spending on all voters or on those who voted for a campaign by matching finance reports with election returns. What conclusions emerge from these numbers?

Campaign strategy is usually more accessible to researchers than are finances. The circumstances of each campaign determine much of the planning. Did a local election occur at the same time as state and national contests or was it separate? If the former, was it a presidential year or "off" year election? Was it partisan or nonpartisan, primary or general? Did an incumbent run for reelection, a challenger oppose an incumbent, or two candidates vie for an open seat? Consider the office sought and what voters expected of that particular office. For example, residents likely looked for different traits from a county sheriff than from a Board of Education trustee.

What choices did a specific local campaign make? Did it, for example, ride the coattails of a political party or other candidates? Or did it take an independent or even oppositional stance? Did the campaign appeal to all voters? Or did it concentrate on some areas or population groups and neglect others? If so, why? Did it emphasize a candidate's personal traits? Or did it stress issues? If the latter, which ones? Did the campaign select local issues or adopt state, regional, or national themes? Was the campaign's approach positive, advocating one or more proposals or claiming credit for current conditions? Or did the campaign attack the status quo or cultivate voters' fears? Did it rely on grass-roots citizen participation or play up support of prominent individuals or groups? Each answer uncovers not only the history of a particular campaign but also reveals much about the community in which it occurred.

While some campaigns work within the existing electorate, others try to enlarge it by registering new voters. Did a local candidate or ballot proposal campaign do a voter registration drive? Why or why not? If so, did it target specific groups of people? Who and why? How did the campaign locate and sign up new voters? Comparing census and voter registration data helps gauge results of registration drives. Besides candidates and political parties, who else recruited new voters in a community? Why did they do this? Did registration drives affect election results? Did they change local politics in other ways?

Consider what a local campaign communicated to the public. Did it make broad, general appeals or send specific messages to particular segments of the community? Campaigns' messages served different

Campaign publicity documented candidates' strategies. This billboard, posted by Dearborn, Michigan, Mayor Orville Hubbard in 1957, mentions incumbency. Its "Keep Dearborn Clean" motto could have appealed to civic pride, referred to Hubbard's resistance to blacks, or both. The comment added to the lower corner, however, indicates that Hubbard was not without critics. *William L. Mills Papers, Box 2, Bentley Historical Library, University of Michigan.*

Voter registration drive, Chicago, 1973. What were voter eligibility requirements and registration procedures in a local community? Did state or provincial government set them? What authority did local officials have? Was it easy or difficult to become a voter? What barriers existed based on gender, age, race, length of residence, and advance registration? What assumptions lay behind each obstacle? How did the national government change the local electorate? One could analyze the impact any or all of the following made on local politics: female suffrage, eighteen-year-old vote, 1965 U.S. Civil Rights Act, poll tax abolition, and the Motor Voter Act. *National Archives, Record Group 412, Environmental Protection Agency, NWDNS-412-DA-13806.*

purposes. One was to convince voters to switch sides or move from undecided to positive. Though few voters changed their minds, in close elections these "persuadables" could determine the outcome. How did a campaign try to convince these voters? Another goal of campaigns was reinforcing supporters' loyalty. This might encourage loyalists to talk up the campaign to family and friends, inspire some to donate time or money, and increase the number who voted. Finally, some political communication discouraged opponents from voting. Intimidation did this directly. Negative campaigning did it indirectly by disgusting people so much that they became politically inactive or even refused to vote. Campaigns targeted negative appeals to likely opponents. Did a local campaign do this? If so, what was the content and the intended audience? How successful was a campaign at delivering each type of message?

Another area of inquiry is how campaigns contacted voters. Local custom, cost, technology, number of campaign workers, and their judgments about what worked each shaped how candidates reached residents. Competition, too, influenced what campaigns did. If Jones broadcast radio ads, Williams may have followed suit. List the different ways a local campaign touched voters. Which methods did it use the most? Which were secondary? What explains these choices? Did opposing candidates or campaigns use the same mix? If not, explain why. How could one judge the success of differing kinds of communication?

Traditionally, personal, face-to-face contact with voters was a vital

Lawn signs on behalf of Polish-American candidates in South Omaha, Nebraska, 1938. Local campaigns that did not buy radio or television advertising could use lawn signs to promote their cause. Signs targeted specific areas, reached every passerby, and, in large quantity, demonstrated strong support for candidates or ballot issues. FSA-OWI Collection, LC-USF33–001278-MI, *Library of Congress.*

element of local campaigns. Historians can probe this topic by examining a single campaign or gauge change over time by comparing recent campaigns to those in the more distant past. Did campaigns hold parades and rallies to inspire the faithful and show their numbers? Did candidates host picnics and barbecues to prove their generosity? What type of contact did campaign workers make with individual voters? Did they go door-to-door, distributing handbills and telling residents about the party's slate? Did they telephone voters? Candidates themselves also may have met voters individually, door-to-door, and in small group receptions. They may also have appeared at churches, clubs, sports contests, county fairs, school events, factory gates, and anywhere else people gathered. In such encounters, how much conversation was about issues? How much was "small talk" to build or reinforce personal ties? Was there appeal to party loyalty? Personal contact by candidates and volunteer workers connected residents to city hall or the county courthouse. It allowed them to tell politicians what they thought, giving candidates valuable feedback. And it increased the number who voted on election day.

Researchers of local political history should also consider printed campaign materials at archives or in personal collections. Look for flyers or handbills that were mailed, given to voters or left at their doors. Also try to locate cards, buttons, stickers, ribbons, pencils, or key chains bearing candidates' names or images. Campaigns also produced signs, ranging from small posters for rallies and windows to larger yard signs and billboards erected on vacant lots and along major streets. Which campaign artifacts survived most often? Which survived the least? Why?

It is useful to study the style and content of printed campaign materials. What colors dominate? What did these colors represent? In the United States, red, white, and blue, colors of the nation's flag, symbolize patriotism. In the 1970s, green stood for environmental sensitivity. What colors are absent. Why? Observe campaigns' use of photographs, logos, and other visual images. What was their content and purpose? How did politicians use partisan symbols? Notice type size and style of printed matter. Did brochures or handbills have few or many words? Did campaign materials emphasize candidate name recognition? Partisanship? A specific issue? The candidate's personal style? An approach to governing? What messages are missing? Although historians can rarely recreate discussions of campaign strategy, printed materials tell them much.

Technological change is as significant to political campaigns as it is

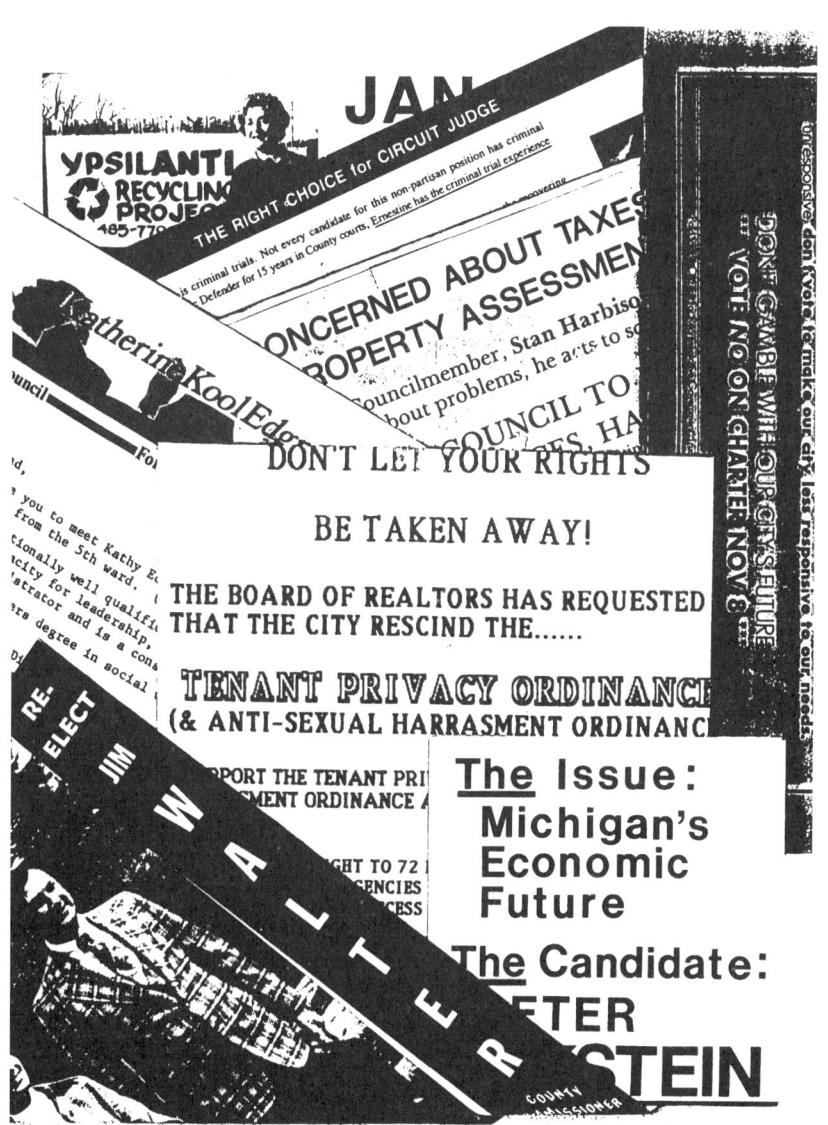

Campaign brochures, flyers, and cards convey candidates' assumptions about motivating and persuading voters. *Author's collection.*

to government. One can emphasize this theme in local political history by describing new methods and analyzing their impact. For example, as the decline of patronage and lessening interest in politics thinned the ranks of campaign workers, technology made mass mailings practical. Computer databases and high-speed printers put names and addresses on labels or flyers. Mailmerge programs produced personalized letters. How did such a development change politics in a community? What did campaigns and voters gain? What did they lose?

Another technological shift was the rise of the mass media—newspapers, radio, and television. As political parties withered, television increasingly shaped public perceptions of candidates and campaigns. The mass media were most influential in state and national elections but also made their mark on local contests. One way they did this was through campaign advertising. Examine newspaper advertising or obtain tapes of political commercials from broadcast stations or from campaign workers. Ask questions about content and style mentioned in the discussion of printed campaign materials. How much advertising occurred? Did it happen throughout a campaign or concentrate at the end? How big were the ads? What was their design and purpose? Note the choices campaigns made among name recognition, issues, and endorsements by notables or by ordinary residents. Did ads attack or rebut opposing campaigns? Estimate the effectiveness of local campaign advertising.

Most newspapers print letters to the editor, and surveys show the public reads them. Some people submitted letters about candidates and elections on their own. Campaigns also encouraged supporters to do so, sometimes even providing letters to loyalists who sent them as their own. Did local campaigns spread their message this way? If so, did their letters to the editor repeat major themes or cover new ground? Did opposing campaigns use letters to the editor? Did editors print all such letters or use them selectively?

Historians of local politics can also examine media news coverage and editorial endorsements of candidates and ballot proposals. As researchers look at evidence, they should consider candidate-media relations. Politicians courted editors and reporters through visits, background information, press releases, press conferences, and attention-getting events. When incumbents announced state grants or challengers invited opponents to debates, released embarrassing reports, or sued adversaries, they hoped for well-timed news stories. The news media snapped at the bait, eager for controversy that would get

Tracing Local Campaigns and Elections 141

people to buy and read papers or tune in local television or radio. The larger the press circulation or broadcast ratings, the more profits mass media would derive from commercial advertising. Meanwhile, publishers, editors, and reporters decided the tone and amount of campaign coverage, based on a mix of their own judgment and their sense of public perceptions.

These factors can be useful to remember when reading newspapers or playing radio or television tapes to see how the media covered a local political campaign. How accurately did media images reflect campaign realities? How did those images shape reality? What did the media say was "news"? How did these stories become news? What information about candidates, issues, and the campaign did the media omit or minimize? How did the media balance news judgments with commercially attractive images? In depicting the campaign, did various media outlets differ or imitate each other? What accounts for such similarities or differences? What was the mass media's impact on how voters thought and acted? How did media images influence election results? How did the media shape relations between citizens and local government?

By the late twentieth century, public opinion polling became common in state, provincial, and national campaigns and appeared in some local elections as well. Professional firms and campaigns each did polling, and several types of polls existed. Most surveyed representative samples of voters at various stages of campaigns to learn how people responded to issues and candidates. Campaigns could then modify what they said and to whom they said it. A second type of polling, the focus group, consisted of small gatherings assembled to talk about candidates, tactics, or policy options. Did local campaigns do polling? Why or why not? If they did, how did they use the information? What difference did polling make in the campaign or election outcome?

The canvass was the oldest and most common type of poll. Whereas polls questioned carefully selected samples, canvasses tried to survey every voter or household in a candidate's district. With voter preference information from the canvass, a campaign encouraged supporters to vote on election day, gave the undecided more information, and ignored opponents. Formerly done by house-to-house visits, canvasses now usually occur by volunteers telephoning from campaign offices or homes. Did a particular local campaign canvass voters? If so, how did it occur? How successful was the canvass? How did the campaign use what it learned?

Campaign rallies and parades, like this march on behalf of Chicago Mayor Richard J. Daley in 1959, reminded voters an election was nearing, demonstrated a candidate's strength, and generated enthusiasm among adherents. Not all of these marchers, however, appear excited. *Chicago Historical Society, Photo Files, ICHi-25553, Chicago Sun Times photograph.*

ॐॐॐॐॐ

A CITY COUNCIL CAMPAIGN IN A SMALL NEW JERSEY CITY

In his campaign handbook, *Getting Elected: A Guide to Winning State and Local Office,* Massachusetts state legislator Chester G. Atkins briefly described several successful grass-roots candidacies. In 1971, David Waks, a young attorney, sought the fifth ward city council seat in Wayne, New Jersey, a city of 52,000 near Paterson. Waks had worked in local Democratic politics, campaigning for Minnesota Senator Eugene McCarthy for president in 1968, helping run a mayoral campaign, and winning election to the Passaic County Democratic Committee in 1969.

An apartment renter, Waks also helped start a tenants' organization that became his political base. Besides tenants' rights, which attracted the many renters in the district, Waks wanted to slow Wayne's commercial development to protect its environment. Though a few volunteers designed and distributed three flyers before the primary, Waks's campaign consisted mainly of his own door-to-door efforts. He spent only $459 on the June primary, and most of this was his own money. His personal efforts, tenant support, and endorsement by reform Democrats carried him to a 422–302 primary victory.

For the November general election, Waks targeted apartment renters for an intensive voter registration drive which added over 500 new voters. As before, he emphasized his own door-to-door campaigning. He recruited about eighty volunteers but still spent modestly, funding most of the $1,450 general election budget himself. As Waks campaigned, he compiled a list of 1,000 voters who promised to back him. On election day, his crew worked his ward's apartment complexes, calling voters on his list. Waks's targeting, popular issues, dedicated personal effort, and effective election-day operation paid off. Waks won the council seat with 1,424 votes, well ahead of both his Republican opponent, who had 898, and the Democrat he beat in the primary, who ran as an independent and finished third with 480.

Source: Chester G. Atkins, *Getting Elected: A Guide to Winning State and Local Office* (Boston: Houghton Mifflin, 1973), pp. 178–183.

ॐ ॐ ॐ ॐ ॐ

Even during a local campaign, some residents had already voted by absentee ballot. Who was eligible to vote before election day in a province or state? Typically, the elderly, physically disabled, and those expecting to be away on election day could vote absentee. In the 1990s, a few states increased voter turnout by making it easier to vote in advance or by mail. A worthy topic is the attention a local campaign gave to absentee voters. Which voters did it target and what steps did the campaign take? Who obtained absentee ballots? How many returned them? What proportion of all voters used absentee ballots? What impact did these voters have on the election result? City, township, or county voting records can disclose the answers.

Historians should also try to reconstruct election-eve campaign efforts. As the election neared, campaigns organized operations for the big day. Meanwhile, they reminded supporters to go to the polls, hanging cards on doorknobs or making phone calls. Some did this in areas where they were strong, while others worked marginal or "swing" precincts. These late contacts increased voter turnout, reinforcing loyalists and swaying a few of the undecided.

Election day was the campaign's climax, and it would end in celebration or disappointment. An account of how a community conducted elections would be worthwhile. What election procedures did state or provincial law prescribe, and what authority did local officials have? On what days and times did local elections take place? Some countries hold elections on Sundays, but voting in the United States and Canada occurs on work days. Canadians receive time off from work to vote, but U.S. employees do not. Who benefits and who loses from this? Were local elections separate from or at the same time as state and national contests? The latter choice saved money and enhanced voter turnout, while the former kept local and national politics apart. Which did a community choose and why?

Next, how were votes actually cast? In the nineteenth century, political parties printed ballots, and people voted their preferred "ticket." Each party's ballot had visible differences; people who wanted to support candidates from both parties needed more than one ballot. By the late nineteenth century, governments authorized official paper ballots. They took a long time to count, and purposeful or accidental inaccuracies occurred. Corrupt election workers could also misplace or destroy ballots. In the twentieth century, voting machines minimized cheating and made election results available quickly. But voting machines were costly to buy, move, and maintain. By the late twentieth century, technology again altered voting procedures, as officials introduced punch cards and optical scanners. What voting technologies has your locality used? How well has each functioned?

While local officials conducted elections, campaigns did their best to win them. Whether a campaign finished with smiles or tears might depend on how it spent its longest day. What did campaigners do on election day? Did their activities derive from local custom? From a campaign's strength or weakness? Or from how competitive each election was? What difference did election-day activity make? How would one go about making such a judgment?

It can be fascinating to trace a local campaign's election-day operations. What did it do at polling places in the district? Often campaigns placed candidate signs outside the building where people voted. In addition, campaigns might station volunteers near the polls to greet arriving voters and give them a card listing favored candidates. These poll cards especially benefited candidates for local or minor offices. This is because voters were less likely to be firm in their preferences for those positions and often would fail to vote for minor offices

Signing in to vote, Grand Rapids, Michigan, 1950s. Find out about local voting locations and procedures. Where did your city or township hold elections? In public buildings? In privately owned halls? In residences? Who chose these sites? What was the significance of each location? How convenient were these sites? For example, tenants in large apartment buildings might vote where they lived, while rural residents often had to go a long distance to cast their ballots. *Paul G. Goebel Papers, Box 9, Bentley Historical Library, University of Michigan.*

Poll workers, Cicero, Illinois. As long as people vote at polling places, governments will employ poll workers. Who staffed polling places? How did officials choose poll workers, and what were their duties? Were they impartial? Did each precinct's poll workers include members of both political parties? Was such representation genuine or nominal? *Chicago Historical Society, Photo Files, ICHi-30842.*

unless reminded to do so. Meanwhile, inside the polling place, other campaign workers, called watchers, checkers, or challengers, kept an eye on precinct election officials and on opponents' volunteers. They might challenge people they believed supported the opposition and were ineligible to vote. Most important, they recorded the name of every voter, so the campaign knew who had appeared throughout the day. From time to time, still other campaign workers, known as runners, retrieved watchers' lists of those who had voted.

Back at campaign headquarters, runners submitted their voter lists, so the campaign knew which supporters had not yet been to the polls. Such missing persons got reminders and offers of rides, child care, or other aid to vote. Some campaigns sent workers door-to-door in areas where support was strong to bring everyone to the polls. They used soundtrucks, bands, or other attention-getting techniques. In some places, parties or candidates gave their forces election-day "running around money" to pay for their time and to fund inducements to reluctant would-be voters. Experienced campaigners knew the daily rhythms of their community and schedules of many voters. Mrs. D'Allesandro, a housewife, voted at midmorning as she took her young children for a stroll. Stan Burkowitz left the factory at 4:00 and stopped at the polls on his way home. And old man Pennington couldn't be bothered with voting unless promised a free brew at the corner saloon if his name appeared on the poll list.

Interviews can partly reconstruct election-day drama, but official records are also useful. Clerks keep poll lists recording voters' names

Election night, William Hale Thompson mayoral campaign, Chicago, 1927, when, despite female suffrage, politics was mainly a male pastime. This crowd of formally attired supporters of ex-mayor Thompson looks glum. But their man prevailed, ousting the Democratic incumbent to win a third, non-consecutive term. *Chicago Historical Society, Photo Files, DN-083173.*

in the order they appeared at the polls. Precinct-level election returns give candidates' tallies and the total number of voters at each polling place. Researchers can calculate turnout rates by comparing these figures to the total registered. Actual participation was higher, however, since registration lists included many who had moved. One can also match precinct-level election data with census tract maps to learn how education, renting, homeowning, race, and ethnicity shaped voting behavior. It is also possible to sample individual voting records to measure how age, gender, length of residence and other factors affected voter turnout. These sources will likely demonstrate what campaigns learned from experience: different types of people took part in politics in different ways.

As election day wore on, campaign teams learned how things were going. At closing time, challengers watched poll workers count paper ballots or open voting machines to reveal the numbers. Loyalists gathered at headquarters or at the hotel, restaurant, or union hall where they would mark the campaign's end. Numbers posted on walls made the crowd festive or morose. Reporters with note pads or microphones asked candidates predictable questions. Winners and losers thanked their supporters, explained the results, and looked to the future. Crowds backing badly beaten hopefuls thinned early, while winners partied late. And close contests kept followers well into the night, awaiting returns from the last few precincts or the absentee counting board. Finally, with all the totals reported and with emotions spent, exhausted campaigners went home to sleep, leaving behind the litter of a long night and a long campaign.

SUGGESTED READINGS

Much of the historical work cited previously mentions the campaign process. But one can also profit from books about political campaigns. The classic title, which still merits careful attention, is Frank R. Kent, *The Great Game of Politics* (Garden City, NY: Doubleday, Doran, 1936). First published in 1923, Kent's book reflects the urban world of organization politics from which Kent came. Two antiwar activists of the 1960s produced a fine pair of how-to campaign guides. Massachusetts state legislator Chester G. Atkins wrote *Getting Elected: A Guide to Winning State and Local Office* (Boston: Houghton Mifflin, 1973), and Chicago reform alderman Dick Simpson gave us *Winning Elections: A Handbook in Participatory Politics* (Chicago: Swallow Press,

1972). A trio of current campaign manuals are political scientist Daniel M. Shea's *Campaign Craft: The Strategies, Tactics, and Art of Political Campaign Management* (Westport, CT: Praeger, 1996), Washington State and King County legislator R. R. Bob Greive's *The Blood, Sweat, and Tears of Political Victory . . . and Defeat* (Lanham, MD: University Press of America, 1996), and a collection of articles edited by political scientists James A. Thurber and Candice J. Nelson, *Campaigns and Elections American Style* (Boulder, CO: Westview Press, 1995). Richard Armstrong, *The Next Hurrah: The Communications Revolution in American Politics* (New York: William Morrow, 1988), addresses direct mail, computers, cable television, and other facets of transforming technologies. To follow current trends, sample *Campaigns and Elections.*

PART IV
DISPLAYING RESULTS

Chapter 7

ILLUMINATING CITY HALL

This final section offers suggestions of how to turn research into a finished work of history. It covers using sources, taking notes, organizing material, writing, and presenting findings. It also refers to guidebooks that give more detailed assistance about each of these tasks.

Most people who attempt it enjoy local history research. Like miners panning for gold, they celebrate each precious nugget of information they find. Encountering the past through interviews, newspapers, magazines, letters, and photographs reveals a world different yet connected to their own. As they do research, historians also meet new people and go places they have not been before. Though some residents, public employees, librarians, or archivists may be grouchy, busy, or unable to help, most are pleasant, eager to assist, and encouraging. As boxes of notes fill, local historians not only learn a lot themselves but also think about how to share their findings with others. Local history efforts do indeed enlarge human knowledge.

Each source deserves thoughtful, precise attention. Historians first make judgments about how the information they find relates to what they are doing. If a historian's main research question is why the Bellingham, Washington, city council bought motorized fire engines, then evidence about the spatial dimensions of Bellingham, its municipal budget, previous fires, and the proportion of wood buildings all would fit this inquiry. Results of Bellingham's previous election, however, are relevant only if it affected the decision. It is best to ignore everything unconnected with the chosen topic, however fascinating it may be. On the other hand, researchers should consider connections that may not be apparent at first glance. For example, perhaps unusually dry weather that presented fire hazards might have contributed to Bellingham's shift from horse-drawn to gasoline-powered pumpers.

Chapter 2 has already pointed out how important it is to think skeptically and critically about historical sources. In daily life, information does not appear randomly; what we hear from others, read, or see on television or the Internet is not an impartial or unbiased group of "facts." Rather, the information stream reflects the choices and purposes of those who contribute to it. This was no less true in the past. Just because a document is old, government-issued, ostensibly "objective" (such as a list or group of statistics), or one with which the researcher agrees does not exempt it from critical inquiry. As Chapter 2 specifies, for every newspaper article, letter, report, directory, diary, or photograph, skillful historians ask essential questions. Who produced this evidence? Under what conditions and circumstances? What were the author's opinions and motives and how did these factors shape the source? For whom was it intended? Were the document's authors first-hand observers? If so, what was their vantage point? What does the source omit and why? How accurate is it? Do other sources confirm or contradict this document? Where does most of the evidence lead? Does the source meet the test of common sense? Is the document authentic?

As historians use primary sources, they follow certain practices. First, much of the evidence from the past is unique or rare, and all of it is valuable. Therefore, researchers handle documents carefully, so they leave no marks, creases, or stains. Historians also keep documents in precisely the same order in which they found them, so others can use them readily. They should not remove archival items, since this would deny them to others. Some libraries permit photocopying, and this can save archival time. It delays note taking until later but does not eliminate that step. Some archives require permission to quote from their materials; save and observe written rules on this matter. Finally, historians record and cite the exact title, date, and location of each document they use so readers of source notes can examine original sources if they wish.

Note taking requires thought, precision, and consistency. Historians make at least two types of notes. One kind is a series of separate bibliography note cards or slips of paper for each source. Small 3" × 5" cards or slips work well. For books, complete citations have author or editor, title, publisher, and the place and date of publication. Including library call numbers helps to locate books easily. Periodical citations give the author and title of an article, name of the magazine or journal, volume number, date, and page number. Newspaper references provide the paper's name, date, and page on which the article appeared. Archival citations identify each document and give its location, collection, and name of the archive. The researcher can enhance the usefulness of bibliography cards or slips by briefly describing each source.

Illuminating City Hall

The second category of notes records the evidence. It is ideal for these, too, to be on identically sized cards or slips of paper. This enables researchers to sort cards and slips in various ways, so organization of information will be as efficient as possible. For this reason, bound notebooks or 8 1/2" × 11" paper are unsuitable. Commercially made 4" × 6" or 5" × 8" note cards or slips are available; cutting 8 1/2" × 11" paper in halves or thirds also makes suitable note slips. To arrange material easily, only one subtopic goes on a note card or slip. For the same reason, use just one side of a note card. It also makes sense to place two headings at the top of each note card: a brief subject summary ("Councilman Olsen opposes fire truck purchase") and a short source citation (*Courier*, 2-17-21, p. 1). Historians do not organize notes by source but instead arrange them according to their project's outline, be it topical, chronological, or a combination of the two. Colored tabs, paper, or cardboard markers keep notes about each subtopic separate. It is wise to store notes in a latched box to keep them secure and in order.

Many researchers find laptop or desktop computers ideal for taking notes. Some rely on word processing programs, while others use programs specifically designed for taking and managing research notes. Whatever the choice, it should offer the precision, access, and flexibility of the system described above. Wise computer users back up their work on a spare disk or hard drive so lost or damaged disks or hard drive failures do not fatally wound their work.

What goes on note cards or slips? Some researchers record their own questions, ideas, and plans to organize a topic. Other notes report how previous historians have interpreted their subject. Most notes, though, record evidence about their topic. Depending on each source, some evidence notes may summarize information; some may record a few specific facts; still others can follow a rich vein of material in great detail. For every source note taken, it is crucial that researchers make a conscious choice to do one of the following two things. Either summarize the source entirely in their own words or copy the source exactly and enclose what they have copied in quotation marks. They should always remain aware of which of these two methods they are using. Those who do not can find a source's words appearing as their own in their finished work. That is plagiarism, the fraud of claiming credit for someone else's creativity. Plagiarism will invalidate your work when someone discovers it.

As historians do research, they make and frequently revise an outline of how they want to organize their work. This outline makes a well-structured and purposeful result more likely. Questions about the past shape the outline. Why did a trend or event occur? How did it happen? What were its results? What conflicts took place and how did people resolve them? What changed and what remained the same? It makes sense to state the major questions at the outset and use those questions to guide research. For instance, why did the city's police officers unionize, and how did collective bargaining change the department? Also researchers should be sure to make clear the significance of their questions. A convincing way to do this is by linking historical inquiry to current concerns. Perhaps the police chief recently resigned owing to conflict with his officers. Or the police union is celebrating its twentieth anniversary. History with a compelling purpose attracts attention, but a project that merely narrates or describes the past may not.

Next the researcher should give the audience context for the selected topic. A historian does well to briefly describe the community, including its location, geography, economy, and population. It is also good to specify the legal and political framework in which a topic occurs. If, for example, the subject is a history of police unions, it makes sense to state the size and composition of the force, the department's administrative structure, and the status of organized labor and collective bargaining in the area at the time the story unfolded. Although historians should provide enough context so readers can understand the findings, giving so much that it obscures the purpose and evidence would be distracting. Thus, relating the rise of labor unions in North America and the entire history of policing would be excessive.

The largest portion of an outline displays the evidence that answers the initial questions. There is no single formula for this. Chronology works best for some subjects, while others benefit from a topical approach. These systems may be combined as well. Whatever the choice, the outline should be clear and logical. Include every major subtopic a reasonable person would expect to find. For example, in an outline on the history of police unionization, include not only police officers, city administrators, and elected officials but other unions and public opinion, even if there are no notes on either. Putting these two things in the outline is a reminder to search for evidence about them. By making the outline determine the evidence, not the other way around, the historian, not the most convenient sources, shapes the result. It is logical to end an outline with a conclusion. Conclusions remind the audience of the point of the study, draw together its most significant findings, and explain why this history helps people understand a community today.

As historians near the completion of their research, they begin to turn outlines into full presentations. Although historians display their work in varied forms, writing is still the most common way they communicate. Good writing requires awareness of the audience and fair treatment of the subject. The most prudent approach is to write for curious, literate, intelligent people who lack specific knowledge about a topic. Explain things nonspecialists are unlikely to know, such as how a city's police department was structured or the length of patrol shifts. In addition, skillful historians treat their subjects with a mix of respect and critical intelligence. First, although it is necessary to make judgments, verdicts should be fair. Fairness entails recognizing the context in which the subjects lived, since their time and place shaped what they thought and did. Fairness also calls for researchers to remember that life is complex, and that neither lavish praise nor cascades of blame suit most situations. Thus, temperate language is more convincing than florid rhetoric. Second, good historians are honest with themselves about their biases and make these views clear to readers. Finally, fairness requires that researchers include and account for evidence that challenges their arguments, not just information that supports their views.

Proficient writing is also a necessary skill for historians. A good way to learn to write well is by reading extensively, especially work by other historians. Most writers find that a computer word processing program is most efficient, for it makes revising their work faster. Paragraphs, sentences, and words are three elements of writing, and we shall consider each here. Every paragraph has a topic sentence (usually the first sentence, sometimes the second) stating its theme. Paragraphs are unified and deal with just one subtopic. The writer develops paragraphs fully by following up topic sentences with explanation and evidence, such as examples, statistical data, and quotations. Writers who cannot develop a paragraph fully either combine it with another (adapting the topic sentence accordingly) or delete it. Use quotations selectively, since many readers find them tedious, especially if used to excess. Quotations should either express something distinctively or prove an assertion. If a quotation does not do either, the writer should put the material in his or her own words. Transitional language ties one paragraph to the next, so writing flows smoothly.

Sentences are the next largest segment of written expression. Sentences have subjects and verbs. They should appear in logical sequence. Some sentences convey broad themes, while others provide specific evidence that supports generalizations. To sustain readers' interest, vary the length of sentences. Avoid very long sentences, which tend to confuse readers. Thus, split such sentences in two. Likewise, refrain from consecutive very short sentences; join two into one interesting longer sentence for more pleasing results.

Words are the smallest unit of writing. Choose them carefully. Words must be clear and precise if readers in both the near and distant future are to understand them. Avoid slang, jargon, and bias that excludes readers. Use words economically, cutting verbal clutter that adds nothing but bores the audience. Do not say, "There is reason to believe that the great majority of Cuban immigrants who resided in Miami . . ." when "Most of Miami's Cuban immigrants . . ." does the same thing more directly. Avoid passive voice (sentences that omit the "actor"), since it is imprecise and flabby. Replace "Awards were given to the best officers," with "Judges handed awards to the best officers." Use action words like "contended" or "declared" instead of "said." Do not employ the same word repeatedly. Repair grammatical errors: verb tense must be consistent; subjects and verbs must agree; antecedents must match pronouns. Spelling, punctuation, hyphenation, and capitalization must be correct. Researchers do not produce polished writing on the first try and do one or more revisions. They include rewriting time in their schedule. To ease the revision process, reading a rough draft aloud, and asking family members and friends to do the same, will identify writing flaws and substantive problems to correct.

Although historians find personal satisfaction from research and writing, few are content with those activities alone. Most want to share finished work with others. Those undertaking assignments for a school class or sponsoring organization have ready-made venues for their work. But even people who do local history on their own will likely look for ways to show the fruits of their efforts. Friends, family, and informants expect to see the results. And most authors themselves want to put what they have done before the public after spending so much time and energy on a project. Moreover, preparing material for others' eyes helps one organize, clarify, and even sometimes change an approach to a topic.

Opportunities abound for presenting the history of local politics and government. Perhaps a study of municipal parks in Silver Spring, Maryland, began as a school assignment. A student submitted a paper to the instructor or discussed his or her findings with classmates. Here the teacher and friends offered helpful feedback. After completing revisions, the student should plan to share the project with an audience larger than one teacher or twenty or thirty classmates.

Consider outlets where amateur and professional historians publish. These take several forms. A historian who has written a book-length manuscript can contact a local or regional publisher or one whose publication list concentrates on the selected area of interest. Those who believe their manuscripts may merit scholarly attention can submit them to a nearby university press for evaluation.

Most local history, however, consists of shorter, article-length work. Here choices abound. Perhaps a city or county historical society prints a newsletter or bulletin with historical selections. State and regional history journals like *Ontario History* or *Pennsylvania Magazine of History and Biography* may also publish articles; some take a scholarly approach, while others seek a broader audience. Certain nationally circulated journals are also possibilities. These, too, include both scholarly publications like *The Historian,* published by history honor society Phi Alpha Theta, and *American History Illustrated,* which appeals to nonprofessionals. One should also consider periodicals with a topical focus. For example, a Hartford, Connecticut, resident who writes a short history of local streetcar and bus service might send the manuscript to a mass transit magazine, especially if the study links the past to current policy questions. Reference librarians at nearby universities, community colleges, or large public libraries can help identify appropriate journals to which authors can submit work. Indeed, writers may have already identified such outlets as they did research.

Locally published newspapers and periodicals for general audiences are another forum for historians to display their work. Daily and weekly newspapers or municipal newsletters may welcome well-written historical articles with popular appeal. Some communities have monthly "city magazines" with features on local personalities and popular culture. These publications routinely print historical articles, and some may even have regular local history columns or features. Even if writers use scholarly or national outlets, it is a good idea for them to share their efforts with local audiences, too. Some residents may offer corrections or valuable additional information.

A specialized type of research about the past is policy history, which analyzes a public issue of current interest. The history of local government and politics brims with potential for this field. What current problems does local government confront? A rise in crime? Rapid land development that threatens the environment? The need to revive a declining inner city? Perhaps a local institution or organization, be it governmental, business, or nonprofit school or foundation may be willing to sponsor a historical study of an issue of current concern and publish the resulting paper.

The Internet is a rapidly growing way to distribute information. Historians can make good use of the World Wide Web. For example, Carl Smith, who teaches English and American studies at Northwestern University, and the Chicago Historical Society did a virtual exhibit, "The Great Chicago Fire and the Web of Memory" (http://www.chicagohs.org/fire/index.html). In over 350 screen pages, Smith displayed maps, photographs, newspaper accounts, testimony, and artifacts related to the 1871 tragedy. While few can match Smith's efforts and institutional support, many local historians can display part or all of their work on the Internet. Through the Web, one not only can disseminate findings beyond the local community but can also contact people with common interests. Researchers can discuss their work with others, find new information, and compare their community's history with those near and far.

Although historians traditionally have relied on the written word, there are other good ways to show your work. Historians can talk to local organizations that share their interests. Most communities have women's clubs, neighborhood associations, political parties, service organizations, civic groups, church auxiliaries, and ethnic and racial forums. Most of these groups hold regular meetings with scheduled speakers. For example, the Chamber of Commerce or downtown merchants' association might sponsor your talk on how businessmen influenced local politics and government in the past. Showing slides can enhance the appeal of any such presentation.

A temporary visual display is another way to let people know about local history. Perhaps a community has a historical museum or archive. Its director may not only offer display space for a month or two but may also suggest showing items from the museum's collection. But history venues are not the only place to let the public know about the past. Quite a few buildings in a community have display space and a need to fill it with something interesting. A local library, elementary or secondary school, community college, post office, senior citizens' center, city hall, and county building may each have display cases, often in heavily used lobbies or hallways. Any place that draws crowds, from regional shopping malls to sports arenas, may also be good sites for local history displays.

Consider adapting historical research for broadcast. Local radio stations may be willing to interview historians for a news segment, invite them to appear on a call-in program, or feature them on a regularly scheduled public affairs hour. Alternatively, with some technical knowledge and equipment, a researcher may prepare an audiotape with music and several readers for different portions of the script, which can include the words of people from the past. Television also offers outlets for local history. Although it is unlikely that prime-time network stations will air these efforts, public television and community access cable stations are fine outlets for local history. Prepare a videotape, using photographs, drawings, maps, and other visual materials to supplement audio narrative and quotations.

No matter how historians share their work in local history, they should extend its life beyond the day their articles appear in the local newspaper or the two weeks the public library displays their project. In *Nearby History: Exploring the Past Around You,* David Kyvig and Myron Marty offer detailed guidance on how to preserve sources and the finished product for future local historians. Donating a project and source materials to a public or university library or to a nearby historical archive will help promote the study of the history of the city, township, or county. Thus, local historians will enable others, most of whom they will never know, to share the excitement they experienced exploring their community's history.

SUGGESTED READINGS

Jacques Barzun and Henry F. Graff, *The Modern Researcher* (5th ed., Fort Worth: Harcourt Brace Jovanovich College Publishers, 1992), is the classic comprehensive guide to history research and writing. A newer, briefer competitor is Wayne C. Booth, Gregory G. Colomb, and Joseph M. Williams, *The Craft of Research* (Chicago: University of Chicago Press, 1995). William Kelleher Story, *Writing History: A Guide for Students* (New York: Oxford University Press, 1999), is an excellent short handbook. Writing style and documentation are the main focus of Diana Hacker, *A Pocket Style Manual* (2nd ed., Boston: Bedford Books, 1997). See also Anthony Brundage, *Going to the Sources: A Guide to Historical Research and Writing* (2nd ed., Wheeling, IL: Harlan Davidson, 1997), and Mary Lynn Rampolla, *A Pocket Guide to Writing in History* (2nd ed., Boston: Bedford/St. Martin's, 1998). Thomas E. Felt, *Researching, Writing, and Publishing Local History* (Nashville, TN: American Association for State and Local History, 1976); David E. Kyvig and Myron A. Marty, *Nearby History: Exploring the Past Around You* (Nashville, TN: American Association for State and Local History, 1982; 2nd ed., Walnut Creek, CA: AltaMira Press, 2000) are designed for community historians.

INDEX

absentee ballots, 143
administrative officials, 36–39
African Americans: and public employment, 41–44, 45–46, 118–119; and public schools, 51; and police, 55; and waste incineration, 72; and public housing, 80–81; and mass transit, 83–84; political power of, 114–120
alleys, 65
annexation, 27
artifacts: as historical sources, 18, 128, 138
Ashe, Arthur, 34
Asian Americans, 114, 116
Atkins, Chester G., 142–143
Atlanta, GA: mass transit, 82–84; African American mayors, 118–120
attorneys: in local government, 38, 43

ballot access, 131–132
Bayor, Ronald H., 82–84, 105
bibliography citations, 154
blacks. *See* African Americans
boards and commissions, 35–36
Bridges, Amy, 104
buildings: public, 30, 32–33; fire stations, 59; government regulation of, 78–79
business: government aid to, 85; political influence of, 98–99, 110–112, 113, 119–120, 130
busing: white resistance to, 107–108

Canada: local government, 10, 25–27, 36
candidates, 130–131
canvass, 141
censuses, 17–18
Central Park (New York, NY), 66–67
Chicago: Italian and Polish immigrants, 41; African American public employees, 43–44; public schools, 51; political party activists, 99, 115, 142; urban redevelopment, 111; African American politics, 115, 117
city charters: questions about, 10–11; reform of, 102
city directories, 17
city halls, 30, 32, 33
city managers, 36–38, 113–114
civil rights movement, 46, 114–115
civil service, 44–45
clerical and secretarial workers: in local government, 40, 46
community organizations: as historical subjects, 8–9; presenting historical research to, 160
community problems: as historical subjects, 9
conservatism, 120–122
construction codes, 78–79
counties, 25–26
courthouses, 30, 32
courts, 58
crime, 57. *See also* Police

Dahl, Robert, 97
Davis, Susan G., 61
Detroit: infrastructure, 51; police, 53–54; aid to needy, 86; white homeowners, 107; Mayor Coleman Young, 117–118
Detroit Publishing Company, 20
Dorsett, Lyle W., 100–101

elections: as historical subjects, 127; historical sources for, 128; primary, 131–132; ballot access for, 131–132; and campaign strategy, 134; in Wayne, NJ, 143; absentee voting in, 143; campaigns on day of, 144, 146–148; day and time of, 144; voting procedure, 144–146; historical sources for, 147–148
engineers, 36, 38–39
environmental issues, 73
ethnicity: and public employment, 41; and police, 55; and parks, 68–69
expressways, 28–29, 120

financing: public services, 51–52; political campaigns, 133
firefighters: technology, 58; volunteers, 59; professionalization of, 59–60; non-firefighting duties of, 60; work culture of, 60; public attitudes toward, 61
forestry, urban, 64–65

gender: and political participation, 13, 147; and public employment, 41, 43, 55; and police, 52, 55; and parks, 68; and reform politics, 103. *See also* Women.
Gosnell, Harold F., 43–44
government employees: 9, 11, 12, 37; categories of, 39; unskilled, 39–40; clerical and secretarial, 40; professional, 40; and ethnicity, 41; and gender, 41, 43; and race, 41–44; obtaining work as, 43; and patronage, 44; and civil service, 44–45; and unions, 45–47; strikes by, 45–46; in local politics, 113–114
government, local: public views of, 3; importance of, 4–5; as historical subject, 9–10; structure of, 10, 25–27; charters, 10–11, records of, 14–15
government services: decisions to provide, 50–51; distribution of, 51; financing, 51–52
growth: pro-growth coalitions, 110–112; opposition to, 114

Hammack, David C., 97
Harris, Carl V., 97
Hispanics, 114–117
historical sources: 7, 12, 87–88, 105, 106, 123; primary, 13–14, 52, 84, 122; secondary, 13–14, 20; critical view of, 14, 153–154; preserving, 14–15; for campaigns and elections, 128, 147–148; citing, 154; rules for using, 154; government records, 14–15, 128; newspapers, 15–16, 84, 122; periodicals, 16–17, 39, 71, 88, 122; manuscript collections, 17, 42; interviews, 17, 128; city directories, 17; censuses, 17–18; maps, 18; artifacts, 18, 128, 138; visual images, 18, 19
history: definition of, 6; questions about, 6–7, 8, 10; disagreements about, 7; how to organize, 8; limiting subject scope, 9–10; presentation of, 158–161
Horowitz, David A., 106–107
housing: government regulation of, 78–79; public, 79–81
Houston, TX: water supply, 75
Hunter, Floyd, 97

immigrants: and public employment, 41, 42; and police, 55
intergovernmental relations, 27–30
interest groups, 130

Index

Internet: historical sources on, 20; presenting history on, 160
interviews, 17, 128
Italian Americans, 41

Jackson, Maynard, 118–120

Kansas City, MO: Pendergast organization, 100–101
Ku Klux Klan, 106–107

La Grande, OR: Ku Klux Klan, 106–107
La Guardia, Fiorello, 104–105
labor unions: and public employees, 45–47; in local politics, 9, 47
Los Angeles: water supply, 75; Richard Riordan, 121–122

manuscript collections, 17, 42
maps, 18
mass media: and political campaigns, 140–141; presenting history on, 160–161
mass transit: private franchises, 81; public ownership, 81–82; in Atlanta, 82–84
McShane, Clay, 38–39
Memphis, TN: and New Deal, 105–106
Metropolitan Atlanta Rapid Transit Authority (MARTA), 83–84, 119
metropolitan government, 26–27
minor parties, 132
Mollenkopf, John H., 110–111
Monument Avenue (Richmond, VA), 33–34
monuments, 33–34
moral standards: and police, 54–55; and reform, 102; neighborhood protest over, 109
municipal government, 25

neighborhood associations, 108–110
New Deal (1930s), 28, 86–87, 105

New York, NY: police and fire associations, 45; Central Park, 66–67; water supply, 75; Fiorello La Guardia, 104–105
newspapers: as historical sources, 15–16, 84, 122; in political campaigns, 140–141; publishing history in, 159
notetaking, 154–155

ordinance enforcement, 57–58
outline, historical research, 155–156

parks: motives for creating, 65–66; Central Park (New York, NY), 66–67; design of and location, 67; use and control of, 67–69, 70
patronage, 44, 56
Pendergast, Jim and Tom, 100–101
periodicals: as historical sources, 16–17, 39, 71, 88, 122; publishing historical research in, 159
playgrounds, 69–71
police: exclusion of African Americans, 42–43; African Americans as, 43; background of, 52–53; public expectations of, 53–56; community relations and review boards, 55; and politics, 56; professionalization of, 56; and technology, 56; and legal procedures, 56–57; as lawbreakers, 57
policy history, 159
Polish Americans, 41
political campaigns: as historical subjects, 127; historical sources for, 128; and political parties, 128–130; interest groups in, 130; candidates in, 130–131; primary elections, 131–132; third parties in, 132; organization of, 132–133; money in, 133–134, 143; strategy of, 134–137; communication to voters, 134–139, 144, 146–147; and mass media, 140; polls and canvasses, 141;

political campaigns (*cont.*)
  in Wayne, NJ, 142–143; and absentee ballots, 143; on election day, 144, 146–148
political parties and party organizations: questions about, 11–12; and public employment, 44; description of, 99–100, 101; causes of, 100; scope of, 101; decline of, 101–102; as historical subjects, 128–130; third parties, 132
political power: distribution of, 98
politics: public attitudes toward, 3, 97; importance of, 4–5; questions about, 11–12; and police, 56; academic models of, 97–98, 103–104; political organizations, 99–102; reform, 102–103; urban liberalism, 104–105; antiminority, 106–108; neighborhood defense, 108–110; urban redevelopment, 110–112; suburban, 112–114; racial minority, 114–120; conservative, 120–122
poll workers, 146
polling, 141
pollution, 73
Poole's Index to Periodical Literature, 16
poverty: government programs to treat, 84–87; causes of, 85–86
primary elections, 131–132
primary sources, 13–20, 52, 84, 122
private sector: as service provider, 40, 46–47, 71–72, 73, 86
professional workers: in local government, 40, 43, 46
provinces and states: relations with local government, 27–28
public housing: control of, 79; site selection, 79, 81; tenant selection, 81; architecture, 81
public spaces, 30

racial minorities. *See* African Americans, Asian Americans, and Hispanics

racial segregation, 43
Readers' Guide to Periodical Literature, 16, 122
recreation, 69–71
recycling, 72–73
reform, 102–104
regional government, 26
Reiss, Albert, 57
revenue sharing, 29
Richmond, VA: monuments, 33–34; minority subcontracting, 118
Riordan, Richard, 121–122
Rosenzweig, Roy, 69

San Francisco: urban redevelopment, 110–111
Sanborn Map Company, 18
Schultz, Stanley K., 38–39
secondary sources, 13–14, 20
sewers and sewage treatment, 77–78
Social Science and Humanities Index, 16
solid waste, 50; municipal collection of, 71–72; private contracting for, 71–72; disposal of, 72; reduction and source separation of, 72–73
source separation, 72–73
special purpose districts, 26
states and provinces: relations with local government, 27–28
Stone, Clarence N., 82–84
street lights, 63–64
streets: patterns of, 61; use and control of, 61–62; paving, 62–63; cleaning, 64; protests about, 109
strikes: public employee, 45–46, 120
suburbs: politics in, 112–114
Sugrue, Thomas J., 107

tax abatements, 85
teachers, 40, 43
technology: and police, 56; and firefighters, 58; and environmental quality, 73; in political campaigns, 138, 140

Index

third parties, 132
townships, 25

United States Conference of Mayors, 28, 104
United States government, 28–30, 75, 77, 79, 86–87, 105
unskilled workers: in local government, 39–40, 43
urban liberalism, 104–105
urban redevelopment, 28, 110–112, 120

visual displays: of historical research, 160
visual images: as historical sources, 18, 19
voters: registration of, 134, 136, 143; eligibility of, 136; surveying opinions of, 141; and absentee ballots, 143; election day procedures for, 144–146

Waks, David, 142–143
War on Poverty (1960s), 29, 87
water: supply, 73–75; private firms and, 73; public systems for, 73–74; sources of, 74–75; distribution and financing, 75; quality of, 75, 77; conflicts over, 77
Wayne, NJ: city council campaign, 142–143
welfare state, 84–87
women: and public employment, 41, 43, 55; and police, 52, 55; in politics, 103, 113, 116
Worcester, MA: conflict over parks, 69, 70
writing, historical, 157–158

Young, Andrew, 118, 120
Young, Coleman, 117–118

Zunz, Olivier, 51